Renewing the Countryside

WISCONSIN

W9-AAK-186

RENEWING THE COUNTRYSIDE

WISCONSIN

EDITORS:

Jerry Hembd, Jody Padgham and Jan Joannides

ART DIRECTION AND DESIGN:

Brett Olson

A PROJECT OF

Midwest Organic and Sustainable Education Service

Northern Center for Community and Economic Development
a joint effort of the University of Wisconsin-Superior and University of Wisconsin-Extension

Renewing the Countryside

PUBLISHED BY

Renewing the Countryside

RENEWING THE COUNTRYSIDE — WISCONSIN

Published by	Renewing the Countryside in partnership with Midwest Organic and Sustainable Education Service and Northern Center for Community and Economic Development—a joint effort of University of Wisconsin-Superior and University of Wisconsin-Extension
Editors	Jerry Hembd, Jody Padgham and Jan Joannides
Lead Writers	Jody Padgham, John Ivanko and Lisa Kivirist
Writers	Lorene Anderson, Mark Fondriest, Jo Futrell, Meg Gores, Ann Hanson, Jerry Hembd, Erika Linn Janik, Jan Joannides, Mary Rehwald, Michelle Shaw and Bill Wright
Lead Photographers	John Ivanko and Tom Baker
Art Director	Brett Olson
Editorial Committee	Jerry Hembd, Jan Joannides, Faye Jones, Jody Padgham and Mary Rehwald
Series Editor	Jan Joannides
Supporters	Brico Foundation, Northland College and the W.K. Kellogg Foundation
Printer	Friesens, Printed in Canada
Paper	100 lb. Sterling Ultra Matte, 10% post-consumer waste

ISBN-13: 978-0-9795458-0-1 Cloth
ISBN-13: 978-0-9795458-1-8 Paperback

Library of Congress Control Number: 2007933412

Copyright 2007 by Renewing the Countryside. All rights reserved.
Portions of this publication may be reproduced with written permission from the publishers.
Address inquiries to Renewing the Countryside, 2105 First Avenue S, Minneapolis, MN 55404
1-866-477-1521 · info@rtcinfo.org · www.renewingthecountryside.org

Distributed by University of Wisconsin Press

First Printing

TABLE OF CONTENTS

FOREWORD

Wisconsin's rich agricultural heritage and identity are coupled with a strong and enduring conservation ethic and sense of stewardship for our land and natural resources. *Renewing the Countryside—Wisconsin* clearly shows how these vital traditions continue to shape how we live and work. It showcases people and ideas that are transforming our state—through knowledge, innovation and creativity.

The health and future of Wisconsin's rural, urban and suburban communities are inextricably linked. This book explores such connections in the areas of art, farming, community, culture, ecology, tourism and recreation, business innovation and education. Underlying themes of importance to all areas and people of the state emerge from the stories told here.

The entrepreneurial spirit is alive and thriving in rural areas and yielding new and innovative products and services. Arts and a rural creative economy enhance our quality of life while bolstering our tourism industry. Renewable sources of energy—including wind, ethanol and solar—and purposeful energy conservation are reshaping individual behavior and business practices. Sustainable agricultural practices are complementing the production of local, specialty and organic foods and beverages. Wisconsin-based organizations are providing educational leadership in the Midwest when it comes to renewable energy and organic agriculture.

A rural renaissance is not only possible for Wisconsin, it is already happening. These stories—exemplary in their own right—are examples that just begin to capture the full range of comparable efforts throughout the state. There are lessons to be learned from these stories about our countryside as we work together to grow Wisconsin.

Jim Doyle, Governor, State of Wisconsin

INTRODUCTION

In these pages, we take you on a journey across Wisconsin. The journey weaves through the state's beautiful forests, farmlands and small towns as we search out some of the remarkable people who are building a new, sustainable rural economy. The people we visit are just a sample of many across the state who are developing new enterprises, growing healthy food, fostering the arts and preserving culture in ways that protect Wisconsin's rich natural resources and contribute to its economic viability. Through their innovative work, these people are building the infrastructure for an even better Wisconsin and creating a lasting legacy for future generations.

We've divided this journey not by regions of the state but by different aspects of rural renewal. We begin with a chapter on the arts, showcasing how artists and lovers of the arts are sharing their passion and vision with residents and visitors alike. From hand-crafted Windsor chairs to the throb of guitar strings escaping from under a big blue tent, this chapter explores how the arts are expanding minds, providing entertainment and connecting people to the unique and the interesting in rural areas.

In the next chapter we look at innovative farming enterprises that push beyond traditional models of row crop and livestock agriculture. From fish to vegetable to apple to dairy farms, all the enterprises featured are run with an eye to economic and environmental sustainability. These are stories that tell of the new agriculture that is thriving across the country.

From farming, we move to a chapter of community stories. While these stories would fit nicely under various headings in this book, what lands them here is their base in community building. Whether it's the community of farmers and customers that develop around a vibrant farmers' market or a community coming together to build a performing arts venue, these stories all share the thread of strengthening or reviving relationships for a larger good.

Our next chapter is entitled "Towards a Healthy Planet." We visit the country's first eco-municipality, one of the oldest sustainably managed forests and enterprises that focus on sustaining nature through renewable energy and landscape restoration. From installing wind turbines to greening abandoned industrial sites, these stories show how caring for and about the environment also makes good business sense.

In chapter five we take a peak at sustainable travel and recreation in the state. From bed and breakfasts powered by wind and sun to a heritage tourism initiative showcasing the homegrown and handmade, these stories reveal a deep sense of place and a vision that while we live in a global economy, we must cherish and care for our local resources.

A book about Wisconsin's countryside that doesn't acknowledge food wouldn't be worth its weight in cheese curds. Milk, cheese, beer, brats—Wisconsin is steeped in food traditions that are centuries old. But a new appreciation for locally-grown, sustainably produced food means that people are going to farmers' markets in droves, demanding heirloom tomatoes and asking for the story behind their artisanal cheese. This chapter shows why Wisconsin is a leader in producing some of the nation's best tasting, highest quality foods.

In our final chapter, we talk about some of the incredible organizations that are providing unique opportunities to learn about the latest in sustainable practices—from a program that teaches kids in Milwaukee to grow food to nationally-recognized events that provide training in organic farming and renewable energy. It is no wonder the state is so rich in innovative, ecologically minded entrepreneurs when one looks at the wealth of learning opportunities available.

We hope you enjoy the journey, whether you live on a farm, in a small town, in the suburbs or in a city. We are all intrinsically interconnected—through our air and water, through our history and future, through food and commerce, and through our travel and play.

We hope this book spurs your imagination and gets you talking to your neighbors, families and community and political leaders about these issues. We also hope it changes the way you think about these issues and encourages or, even better, inspires you to make choices that are good for the environment, rural communities and human health.

From the Editorial Committee—Jerry Hembd, Jan Joannides, Faye Jones, Jody Padgham and Mary Rehwald

ARTS & CULTURE

What better place to start looking at Wisconsin's rural renewal than through the lens of the arts. Capturing and reflecting our souls, artists can inspire us to smile, cry, laugh and ponder the depths and wonders of the world around us. And beyond touching our hearts and minds, the arts play an important role in Wisconsin's rural economy.

The stories told here reflect the creative passion, persistence and vision that thrives in our rural communities. Feel the throb of guitar strings escaping from under a big blue tent. Observe the delicate curl of wood grain in a handmade chair. Absorb the myriad inspirations

of a rural arts colony. Follow a meandering trail connecting rural artists to each other and the community that appreciates them.

By developing local talent or bringing in outside artists, rural communities are enriching the lives of local residents and attracting visitors and tourists. In these pages are examples of how, throughout the countryside, the arts are expanding minds, providing entertainment and connecting people to the unique and the interesting. We invite you into the diverse worlds of Wisconsin's rural artistic community, to enjoy the creativity they offer and, perhaps, inspire you to experience and support the arts firsthand.

Weaving a Cultural Tapestry
Folklore Village, Dodgeville

At Folklore Village, they view culture a little differently. It's not just something you find in a museum or an art gallery or at the opera.

"It's really the big and little decisions we make every day—whether to eat together as a family, whether to leave the farm to take a job in the city—all these things combine to create culture," says Doug Miller, executive director of the 94-acre farm and cultural, educational and community center nestled in the rolling hills between Ridgeway and Dodgeville.For example, sharing a meal with family and friends, catching up on the day's news, making plans—things many of us take for granted. But along with other time-honored customs, they are experiences that more and more people never have.

"There is a 'culture of the dinner table' that goes back to our country's roots," Doug explains. "Today we're seeing kids who don't understand the concept of passing a dish around the table. Taking food for yourself and leaving enough for others is not something they're used to. Compare sharing a meal together with the fast-food experience that's the norm for many kids and you have a microcosm of what's happening in our culture," he says.

For more than 35 years, Folklore Village has worked to preserve and strengthen our country's diverse culture by shining a spotlight on folklife learning—what Doug defines as "the things we learn by watching, listening and copying the people around us. It's

important," he continues, "because it defines how we play and celebrate, the foods we eat, the jokes and stories we share, our craft and work skills, our dances and songs, and the values and beliefs we pass on. It's often all but invisible under the tidal wave of mass marketing and commercialism."

Folklore Village aims to help people discover and appreciate their own heritage and traditions and those of others. How? Simply by having fun, says Doug. "When people have fun, they get the best part of what we offer."

The strategy seems to work, judging by the more than ten thousand people per year—thousands of them children—who show up for the candlelight potluck suppers, barn and folk dances, retreats, cooking demonstrations, crafts classes, holiday and seasonal festivals, concerts with music ranging from Cajun to Slovenian polkas to Ojibwa flutes, and myriad other activities— more than one hundred per year all together. Around 90 percent of the events feature live music and almost always include a mix of kids, seniors and adults. Local hotels and musicians also benefit from the steady flow of visitors.

While Folklore Village programs highlight Wisconsin's rural traditions, they also showcase craftspeople and artists from around the world. Art, food, dancing and music speak a universal language that people everywhere can understand.

ARTS & CULTURE

The idea for Folklore Village came from its founder and guiding spirit, Jane Farwell. Since the 1870s, Farwell's family had lived on the farm that makes up the present-day site. Young Jane grew up there in the 1920s and '30s, surrounded by the rural and cultural traditions of her Iowa County home. It wasn't unusual for neighbors to roll back the rug, bring out the fiddle and enjoy an impromptu dance.

But as she got older, Jane noticed that some of the traditions she loved as a girl were being lost to the industrialization that was overtaking agriculture. She went away to Antioch College and in 1938 graduated with honors with a degree in rural recreation leadership. Not long afterward, she decided to put her efforts into preserving and spreading the rural traditions she loved. She became a renowned folk dance teacher, gaining a national reputation, and even toured as a U.S. cultural ambassador to Japan in the 1950s.

In 1967, Farwell bought an abandoned one-room schoolhouse near her farm and, with the help of friends and neighbors, fixed it up for performances. Thus, Folklore Village was born. In the 1980s, Farwell Hall, an airy, barn-red structure with hardwood floors, colorful murals, large windows, a kitchen and space for cultural exhibits was built. It's where most of Folklore Village's gatherings

and events are held today. In 1993, Folklore Village added more space by purchasing and restoring an 1882 church and moving it to the property.

Doug came to Folklore Village in 1991. He worked alongside Jane to create high-quality programs and extend Folklore Village's community and outreach efforts until her death in 1993. Since then, Doug has continued to build on Folklore Village's reputation, adding environmental stewardship to its goals in 2002 with a 40-acre on-site prairie restoration. In a partnership with the U.S. Fish and Wildlife Service, the project is restoring native plants and revitalizing the area as habitat for grassland birds. When it's completed, school children and members of the local community can experience firsthand the prairie ecosystem and its importance for wildlife.

In 2002, Folklore Village embarked on another significant task—the restoration of the 1848 Aslak Olsen Lie house. Lie was a master craftsman, carpenter, cabinetmaker, blacksmith and community leader who lived in Norway and immigrated to the United States.

Once listed on the National Register of Historic Places, the 40-by-17-foot log house had fallen into a state of disrepair. To preserve it for future generations, the home's owners donated it to Folklore Village. It was disassembled piece by piece and moved to the farm where it will be restored and serve as a place where people can appreciate Lie's artistry and his Norwegian culture.

In 2003, Folklore Village won the Governor's Award in Support of the Arts, sponsored by the Wisconsin Energy Corporation of Milwaukee and the Wisconsin Foundation for the Arts. Many local and state businesses, along with private individuals, provide financial support.

Over the years, Folklore Village has faced its share of challenges. Like most nonprofit organizations, it relies heavily on volunteers. "There's a decline in the volunteer time available—especially in a rural area," Doug says. And good leadership can sometimes be hard to find. "The best leadership is when people don't know there's a leader," Doug believes. In fact, he thinks that a place like Folklore Village could be replicated elsewhere if it had good leadership. The key, he believes, is to find a location where people feel respected and nurtured.

Doug likes to talk about the invisible threads that connect us to people and traditions in our past. "There's an old fiddler's tune called 'Soldier's Joy' that goes back to the Revolutionary War,'" he says. "That song has been passed along from person to person to person. We're not just learners—we're also teachers for future generations."

TIMELESS FURNITURE
Baraboo Valley Windsor Chairs, Rock Springs

The quaint workshop of David Ogren lies in the small town of Rock Springs, surrounded by scenic hills and a meandering river. David is crafting a livelihood making fine Windsor chairs and other furniture that find homes in houses spanning the continent. Joining what are possibly as few as 35 Windsor master chair makers in the United States, David's Baraboo Valley Windsor Chairs prospers by the unique intersection of his skilled hands and the far-reaching impact of the Internet. His customers are people who seek the highest quality, superior workmanship and authentic 18th century designs for Windsor chairs—chairs that last for generations.

"What I had to show for a typical 60-hour workweek was a paycheck and a big stack of papers," smiles David, explaining how he went from a 12-year career as a chemist in an environmental laboratory to that of a fine craftsman making early American era furniture in an old renovated garage. His wife, Maria, and their three grown children have played many roles in the entrepreneurial venture, helping out when they could.

"David has a keen eye for design and an ability to match comfort with structure for a truly remarkable chair," shares Maria, who works as a nurse for the St. Clare Hospital as well as a volunteer for numerous other community organizations. "I've used Maria's seat for years to test out my chairs," teases David, who's clearly left behind the stress and angst that once occupied his past career at the wastewater plant lab.

Baraboo Valley Windsor Chairs specializes in reproductions of Windsor chairs, historic chairs originally from England and made in America during the Revolutionary War period. David continues the tradition of being a "chair-wright," using the skills and reproduction versions of the same hand tools used by the craftsmen of the 18th century. Just looking at a Windsor chair, the graceful spindles and lightweight design may appear delicate, but actually the opposite is true of this sturdy design. The creation of a Windsor chair starts with straight-grained wood, hand-hewn (not sawn) directly from the log. After shaping, drying and bending, this "riven" wood is far superior to kiln-dried lumber. It will become the bent backs, arms and spindles of future chairs. This quality, along with mortise and tenon joinery, gives the

chairs, benches and tables great strength for the long haul. Glue and hardwood wedges are used to secure critical joints, but no screws or nails are used in the chairs' assembly. The real job of a chairwright lies in combining all of these skills to create beautiful furniture, sturdy enough for generations of use. "My customers' great-grandchildren will be thinking about whom to pass these chairs on to," explains David.

"I liked working with my hands and it seemed a natural fit. So after subcontracting with the acclaimed local furniture maker J. Scott Allen and building up my confidence and skills over several years, with Scott's encouragement I decided to go out on my own making Windsor chairs," explains David. "I took one introductory chair-

making class at the Windsor Institute in New Hampshire, then started up the business part-time, while subcontracting for a while with Scott and working various other part-time jobs for a few years. I began learning everything I could on my own and built up a collection of useful references for acquiring skills ranging from splitting tree trunks to advanced woodturning to chair design." As questions or problems came up, David either figured them out on his own or consulted with other chair makers through a "Windsor Chair Resources" website that also now connects to his website.

David uses locally grown hardwoods and softwoods. Softwoods such as pine, basswood or poplar are hand carved to make the seats. Maple or birch hardwoods are typically used for turned parts such as legs and armposts. The back spindles and bent arms and backs are made from hardwoods such as hickory or red oak that have superior bending qualities. David often scavenges downed urban or farm trees that would normally end up rotting in a brush pile or in someone's wood stove for these parts. The typical Windsor design takes advantage of the best qualities of three to four types of wood. For this reason most chairs were and still are painted and finished with a milk paint or oil finish, though David does make chairs and other furniture that are not painted. The choice of woods, design and construction technique result in a chair that is strong enough to support the sitter yet supple enough to flex with a sitter's movement and seasonal weather variations. "You simply can't get the same results with power tools and off-the-rack lumber," adds David. An early bird by nature, David can often be found amidst the sawdust in the shop at dawn, working for a few hours before breakfast.

While the quality and workmanship of the chairs speak for themselves, it's the Internet that makes the business viable—and profitable. "Getting listed on websites that people often go to for information on fine furniture was key," says David, about how he started to harness the power of the Internet to propel his business forward and successfully prospect for new customers and projects. He created the Baraboo Valley Windsor Chairs website using a relatively simple website generation program (homestead.com) and opened up his business on-line with only a $300-a-year investment. "I also learned some tricks," adds David, "like making all my product photographs in low resolution so they load fast and using keywords that those who would be interested in what I make might use themselves."

About 80 percent of David's business now comes through the Internet. The remaining 20 percent, not surprisingly, comes from satisfied customers and their referrals. Complementing the Internet is cost-effective shipping that allows him to ship anywhere, anytime, on time. The chairs are much lighter than typical furniture. Smaller

stools can often be shipped via FedEx or DHL. Shipping a chair or set of chairs gets more complicated but will generally cost about 10 to 12 percent of the purchase price for shipment. David himself delivers orders within a 250-mile radius for a small fee. Large sets usually require contracting with a trucking company, but David and Scott delivered an order of sixteen chairs and two tables directly to Long Island, New York for a substantial savings over the cost of crating and shipping to the client.

"Our customers come looking for handmade furniture, often with a specific design in mind," explains David, recognizing the growing interest in handcrafted items. "It has more character and lasts longer than any factory-made, mass-produced products. Our customers are interested in history and design and intrigued by 18th century style furniture. Everyone picks their own finish for the chairs, and it seems that just about everyone has some form of customization in their order." A typical dinner table set of four Windsor side chairs and two Windsor arm chairs would take about three weeks to complete. Besides its namesake Windsor chairs, the company has crafted stools, benches, tables and high chairs, often working from sketches or photographs provided by customers. Prices start at about $200 for a bar stool and increase rapidly to over $1,000 for a Nantucket fan back arm chair or a settee.

"People really want to know the detail on how we made their chair," adds David. "They want to see and touch the hand tools. They understand that the chairs are made with hands and experience, not a machine in a factory. The more the rest of society keeps on buying cheap, imported, throw-away goods, the more a growing segment of this group will be seeking out quality products that don't just last a lifetime, they last for generations."

"Our customer base in the early years was, geographically speaking, far away," chimes in Maria. "Area residents often commented that they didn't even know we were here. Now more of David's customers are from around home, people who seek to support local artists." David's recent participation in the region's Fall Art Tour—as a guest artist—opened up his workshop for public tours and captured new interest in his distinctive fine furniture. He says, "The Fall Art Tour is helping make those connections amongst artists living in town, and those who are searching for a work of art to grace their homes. The Tour attracts a wide variety of people." The celebration of the arts and artists has emerged over the years in the small town of Baraboo and surrounding communities.

At about the same time the Fall Art Tour started in the Baraboo area, Maria initiated the art exhibit at the local St. Clare Hospital. Like the Art Tour, the hospital exhibit has also become a local community tradition. Experiences like these have created an informal but thriving artisan community. Take as an example their neighbor and good friend, Homer Daehn, master woodcarver, shipwright and irrepressible recycler. David has learned much about woodworking from Homer and they both scout out potential sources of fine wood, actively seeking out downed trees and other wood for each other's projects.

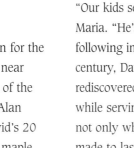

In the spring of 2007, David completed a large commission for the new Aldo Leopold Legacy Center on the Leopold property near Baraboo. The Legacy Center, when completed, will be one of the "greenest" designed buildings in the country. Along with Alan Andersen, who made six oak conference room tables, David's 20 custom designed armchairs are made from the cherry and maple

trees that were thinned from the Leopold land in the process of maintaining the ecological health of the forest.

"Someday I would like to have an apprentice to work with me and learn the trade," admits David, looking to the future. "I'm getting close enough in sales growth to justify hiring someone or subcontracting out some of the work. Perhaps my son, Zach, who's moving back home might join me in the shop," he adds hopefully. Such expansion—tied also to expanded workshop space—would offer David more space and time to pursue his own creative designs for Windsor chairs and other furnishings.

Speaking of expansion, recently David and Maria purchased a small acreage 10 miles west of Baraboo near Rock Springs, Wisconsin. The homestead's classic timber framed barn will be renovated eventually for shop and studio space for the growing business. Their two sons and daughter will play a large part in the development of the new place into a business and home.

"Our kids see what he's created and say 'that's cool'," shares Maria. "He's mellowed out by doing what he loves now." Besides following in the footsteps of the master chair makers of the 18th century, David Ogren and Baraboo Valley Windsor Chairs have rediscovered and rekindled the authentic spirit of a timeless craft while serving the swelling ranks of customers who want to know not only who made the chairs they're sitting on—but how they're made to last forever.

Under the Big Tent
Lake Superior Big Top Chautauqua, Bayfield

The road to Big Top Chautauqua winds uphill through the deep trees next to Lake Superior, far away from bustle, noise and light pollution. Every summer, thousands of people make this drive to see their favorite performers. The night is cool, and the atmosphere around the tent always lively. If the night is clear, you can see the stars, maybe even the northern lights.

As if the preshow dinner of boiled and seasoned Lake Superior whitefish and Leinenkugel's beer isn't enough, the house band at Big Top Chautauqua rocks the crowd with shoe-tapping melodies full of guitar, banjo, fiddle, mandolin and electric woodwind solos. Summer in the Northwoods means nights of great performances at Big Top Chautauqua, Wisconsin's genuine old-fashioned, blue-and-grey, striped tent show.

Now in its twenty-second year, Big Top Chautauqua is a renewal of the historical traveling chautauqua, meant to educate and entertain with lectures, vaudeville shows and musicians. The Big Top's mission to "enhance cultural opportunities and create a sense of community and connection to the life and history of the Upper Midwest" has supported founder and artistic director Warren Nelson in writing and performing 11 original house show musicals that combine stories, songs and historic images. The Blue Canvas Orchestra & Singers—playing together since 1984—accompanies his productions with an original score. Warren has played with members of the Blue Canvas Orchestra since the 1970s.

Big Top's permanent home is at the base of Mt. Ashwabay Ski Hill in Bayfield County. Performers from all over the world come to play—including Greg Brown, Taj Mahal, Dar Williams, The Smothers Brothers and Willie Nelson. New and veteran performers always marvel at the tent: its lighting, surroundings and acoustics. The sound is like nowhere else. Old-fashioned on the outside, the tent is fully equipped with top-of-the-line sound and light systems on the inside.

Still intimate with 900 seats, the padded benches are close to the stage, and the sound is good anywhere you sit. If you listen, laughter always punctuates the murmurs of the crowd before the show. There's a relaxed atmosphere; people come to be taken away with music, dance and theater.

Warren, with his bushy white mustache and sassy tenor voice, leads the crowd in "Ballyhoo!"—his original tribute to the tent, getting the crowd to laugh and yell along. "Is this anyone's first night at the tent? Raise your hands!" He leans in with a smile when hands timidly raise. "Shame on you! Where ya been?"

Musician, actor, composer and poet, Warren, with his partner Betty Ferris, has created a variety of original shows including: *A Martin County Hornpipe*, *Souvenir Views* and *Riding the Wind*—which is about the city of Bayfield. These shows combine historic images, storytelling, dancing, acting and original music to create an

ARTS & CULTURE

entertaining trip through time. Focusing on local history, Warren incorporates lumberjacks, voyageurs, sailors and lighthouse keepers into his shows, giving them voice and remembering their importance in making the North what it is. His newest show, *Old Minnesota*, premiered in his hometown of Fairmont, Minnesota and will tour all over the state. He's been on public radio's *Prairie Home Companion* and has his own radio show of tent performances. *Tent Show Radio* broadcasts on many stations around the country.

"As a showman, I have always wanted a tent show," says Warren. He could have had anything, but he just wanted an all-canvas tent. The tent has since opened every summer, bringing in over 70 locally and nationally known performers each year.

"It's just good people," says Kay Putnam, who has volunteered at the tent with her husband, Don, for 12 years. "We have a lot of fun, and we see a lot of good shows," she says. The Big Top is mostly volunteer-run, from the ticket booth to the ushers, and people just keep coming back. With performances five nights per week from early June through the beginning of September, the Big Top is true Northwoods summer entertainment for locals and tourists alike.

As the Blue Canvas Orchestra & Singers end their upbeat last tune, the crowd claps and laughs, lingering in the after-show buzz before saying goodnight under the wide open sky ... and another night at Big Top Chautauqua comes to a close.

PUTTING CULTURE BACK IN AGRICULTURE
The Wormfarm Institute, Reedsburg

Most folks look at rural acreage, a weather-worn dairy barn and an ample farmhouse and think "farm" in the conventional sense: plant seeds, grow crops, harvest, sell. But Jay Salinas and Donna Neuwirth saw deeper possibilities for their 40-acre farm outside of Reedsburg. Drawing from their personal education and experiential roots in the arts, Jay and Donna created Neu Erth Wormfarm and the Wormfarm Institute, utilizing the farm as an inspirational palette for reconnecting and restoring links between the arts and the land.

Flash back to the early 1990s, when Jay and Donna lived the bohemian lifestyle in Chicago; Jay was making sculpture from urban detritus and Donna was creating avant-garde theatrical props and scenery for special events. "At the time, we lived in a 6,000 square foot old ballroom with 30-foot-high ceilings. We realized our need for space and also realized this was an unusual situation to have access to so much affordable living and studio space in the city," recounts Jay. When their lease for the ballroom was not renewed, the situation prompted Jay and Donna to think creatively about their next steps, which led them to their rural Wisconsin base in 1993. "We didn't have any practical agricultural experience between us," says Donna, "but we were driven by a desire to be more in control of our lives and the things around us. We were ready for something new."

Donna and Jay's passion for connecting people to the land through art now drives the Wormfarm Institute, a nonprofit organization the couple launched in 2000. Based on their Reedsburg farm, the

Wormfarm Institute helps create opportunities for bridging culture and agriculture. The nonprofit drew inspiration from and helped formalize an "artist in residency" program Donna and Jay informally started in the late 1990s. Artists come to the farm for varying lengths of time, from two weeks to six months. Each contributes 15 to 20 hours a week in the garden in exchange for room and board and access to an expanding studio in the old dairy barn. Facilities include a ceramics studio and kiln, electric welding facility, foundry, a shop full of tools and a range of indoor spaces in the various outbuildings that can be used to accommodate creative work. The Wormfarm Institute can host up to four visiting artists at a time and has hosted more than 30 artists over the years, the majority sculptors and ceramic artists but painters, writers and composers as well.

"Having the artists on the farm enriches the experience for everyone," explains Jay. A former visiting artist says it best: "While there, I was working in three different ways: creating my own paintings, contributing to local cultural projects, and helping in the garden. It was gratifying to see how the development of each of these activities was enriched by the influence of the other two. Working in the garden was essential for establishing my vital connection with the earth and to remove the feeling of being just a visitor. It was a key activity for joining with the landscape I wanted to reflect in my paintings. Ultimately, it permitted me to feel a part of what I observed and painted."

The land itself, the rolling green pasture, hills and woods and the vibrant rainbow of colors in the garden, combined with the fact that many of these artists are more urban-based and truly out of their element in such a rural setting, provide a jolt of inspiration and lead them to powerful creative expressions. Sharing their creative work with the local community is a requirement of the residency program. Artists in residence for two months or longer must host an exhibit, performance, lecture or demonstration for the local community. They also are asked to donate a work to the Wormfarm permanent collection, which has grown to over 30 pieces of sculpture, prints and paintings. The Wormfarm space in downtown Reedsburg, The Woolen Mill Gallery, exhibits the visual artists' work. Writers have done readings at a bookstore in nearby Baraboo. Events at the local library have featured a Cuban permaculturist and a Spanish painter. School presentations have included growing micro greens, composting and sustainable agriculture.

Another program area for Wormfarm includes creating community connections to the arts through public events and murals. One of the most successful events that sprouted through Wormfarm in 2004 and continues annually is the summer Reedikulous Puppet Festival, playing off the "Reedsburg" town name and an annual existing city event called Reedikulous Days. This wondrous event provides free, weeklong, giant puppet-making workshops and culminates in a weekend parade and performance. Such community art efforts can unexpectedly, and fruitfully, cross over with the visiting artist program.

In 2004, when the first puppet festival started, Ramon Lopez, an oil painter from Barcelona, Spain, was a visiting artist at Wormfarm. By coincidence, his hometown region is renowned for creating *gegants*, giant life-sized puppets that for 800 years have paraded down the streets. "Ramon admits the gegants were a ubiquitous part of his home life and he hadn't paid much attention to them prior to coming to Wormfarm," explains Jay. But knowing that this puppet festival was happening in Reedsburg, Ramon prepared himself and brought a photo presentation of the Catalonian festival, which he then shared through public presentations at the library and local service clubs.

With support from individuals and businesses and local, county and state grants, Wormfarm works to revitalize downtown Reedsburg through a series of community murals using the talents of local artists to graphically tell the stories of the town's past. Each mural provides an opportunity for community and school participation and has included everyone from high school students to septuagenarians. The first mural depicted the woolen mill, which for decades served as the town's largest industry, one that relied on a flourishing agricultural economy.

Other Wormfarm Institute programs include ways to connect the land with area youth. Artward Bound brings students and teachers from such groups as the Young Women's Leadership Charter School in Chicago and Growing Power in Milwaukee to the farm for several days to make art, learn about sustainable agriculture and meet with area folk artists. "For some, it was their first night sleeping in a tent," smiles Jay. Renewal Gardens, a joint project between the Wormfarm Institute and Renewal Unlimited, an area social service agency, helps young adults gain job and life skills through running a market garden. Receiving a stipend for their work and working as a team with adult mentors, these teens not only garner entrepreneurial experience but can see the end results of their efforts as their high quality, unique garden produce is sought out by high-end restaurants in the Wisconsin Dells resort area.

Renewal Gardens brings together a wide range of partners beyond the program participants and Jay and Donna, including Master Gardeners who serve as mentors and private landowners who donate garden land. "While working in the gardens, these teens not only discover better food, but they learn some of life's larger lessons through agriculture such as patience, delayed gratification and staying focused and on task," adds Jay.

The Wormfarm Institute evolved after Jay and Donna's first years on the farm, during which they jumped into organic agriculture full steam but with minimal growing experience. "Our gardening experience prior to moving to the farm was basically one tomato plant in a five-gallon bucket on the fire escape," admits Jay. Donna and Jay started a small kitchen garden the first year on the farm that quickly sparked their passion for agriculture. "I guess ignorance was our friend those first years on the farm. If we had realized what we were getting ourselves into, we probably wouldn't have done it," Donna says with a smile.

The couple thought they would enter semi-retirement with their decreased income needs; their farm mortgage was one third of what they used to pay in Chicago rent. But that first garden transformed their plan. "As soon as the first seeds started to sprout, we were hooked on growing things," adds Jay. Providing a different backdrop and medium than typical art studios, Donna and Jay found the gardens a fresh creative outlet. "Instead of individual sculptures, I manipulate natural processes providing not only significant aesthetic and conceptual rewards, but good things to eat."

Donna and Jay were early pioneers in urban-rural connections and community supported agriculture (CSA). Intrigued by the upfront payment from food shareholders, they started a CSA business in 1995 aimed at the Chicago market. Yet from the start, this creative pair put their innovative spin on agriculture. Not wanting to make the four-hour drive to Chicago to drop off weekly CSA deliveries, Neu Erth Wormfarm shareholders each committed to coming out to the farm for a weekend each season to pick up that week's produce boxes and deliver the harvest to the Chicago

pick-up site. With a big farmhouse and more space than they personally needed, Donna and Jay converted the second floor into guest quarters for two families, including kitchen facilities for making meals. "This simple idea worked very well with us—way beyond just saving us driving time—because it provided opportunities for our shareholders to both connect with the farm and each other. Our 60 shareholders today see the farm stay as the most valuable part of their CSA package, which has resulted in very loyal members, many of whom have been with us since we started over a decade ago," Donna explains.

With the varied Wormfarm Institute projects and daily responsibilities of the farm, Jay and Donna find their lives creatively full, enriched by the surrounding beautiful landscape and inspiring people. "My definition of success has evolved since coming to the farm," explains Jay. "I measure success by the quality of people I interact with and the unexpected connections to community. Our projects now are off the pedestal and into the world."

THE FALL ART TOUR
Mineral Point, Spring Green, Dodgeville and Baraboo

Since 1994, the Fall Art Tour—a 60-mile route encompassing the communities of Mineral Point, Spring Green, Dodgeville and Baraboo—has lured art collectors and travelers alike, eager to experience first-hand the one-of-a-kind, one-at-a-time treasures crafted by some of Wisconsin's leading and emerging artists. It's an event created by artists for artists and anyone who appreciates art. The event forges relationships between artists and thousands of art buyers and enthusiasts who arrive every year, enhancing the economic prosperity of both artists and non-artists who call these communities home.

Held every third full weekend in October—perfectly timed for the spectacular show of autumn colors—the Fall Art Tour today features more than 50 artists and fine craftspeople who open their galleries, studios and homes to the public during the three-day event. Meandering through the lush countryside, along quiet small town lanes, or nestled amongst scenic coulees, the self-guided tour brings art aficionados face to face with painters, sculptors,

potters, weavers, jewelers, glass artists, woodworkers and fiber and mixed media artists, all busy at work in their studios and eager to converse with visitors on the finer points of their creations.

"We started with a handful of artists from several communities, getting together to reach out to the public by opening up our studios and doing demonstrations," explains Diana Johnston. Among the founding artists of the Fall Art Tour, Diana and her husband, Tom, own the award-winning Johnston Gallery and Brewery Pottery Studio in Mineral Point, where they throw pottery during the tour. "Demonstrations by the artists are the key to our success," continues Diana. "During the tour, craftspeople blow glass, make jewelry, spin wheels and carve wood. The personal connection between artists and participants is what makes it so special."

"It's fun for people to watch the artists work, learn about what goes into each item and understand the whole process," says Diana. "These days, everything has gotten so much the same at the stores where many people shop. But by visiting with artists, often in their studios, people get a very personal experience. They make a connection to the work being created and the person who is making a living doing what they love."

"We were among the first in the Midwest to offer demonstrations of our work as a part of an art tour," echoes Maya Madden, another of the tour's founding artists. She creates No Rules Jewelry, with her husband, Wayne Farra. They also own No Rules Gallery, which features over 50 artists and is located in Spring Green. "It goes beyond just exhibiting our work," Maya says. "People come back year after year. Many buy the art because of their personal connection with the artists. They realize they're buying a piece that is an expression of the artists themselves, and of their skill. This is something that's missing in many people's lives."

The Fall Art Tour capitalizes on the abundance of artists and craftspeople, cast like a web along Highway 23. The scenic countryside and small town life, along with affordable housing and studio space, led many artists to open up their studios and galleries in the region. "It's an easy distance to major markets, like Chicago, Minneapolis and Madison," says Maya, "but we wanted to attract more people with the art tour who would appreciate the quality and uniqueness of our work, and had an interest in our lifestyle. Many of the artists work in interesting places, like an old brewery, farmhouse, historic stone cottage or, like us, in an old one-room schoolhouse."

As the tour grew, so has involvement on the part of local chambers of commerce and businesses, many of which contribute funds toward marketing efforts. Such an outpouring of interest, from outside and within many communities, rekindled a greater support of the arts. The Fall Art Tour received the 2001 Tourism Award from the Baraboo Chamber of Commerce about the same time many residents began to consider the area as an "arts community."

Since the first Fall Art Tour, both the number of participating artists and visiting public have more than doubled. So, too, has the number of communities or regions that have been inspired by the success of the Fall Art Tour, creating similar events of their own. "Competing art tours have sprung up like mushrooms," shares Maya. "Madison now has a couple, as does Galena, Illinois, a group of communities in eastern Iowa and the Coulee Region along the Mississippi."

Due to the success of the tour and to help in securing grant funding support, the Fall Art Tour incorporated as a 501(c)3 nonprofit corporation in 1997. It is managed informally by a nine-member volunteer Coordinating Committee, made up of three artist representatives from each community. This committee is charged with overseeing the marketing of the tour as well as selecting the artists and the tour route. "We've always limited the number of artists per community and the geographic location of the tour," explains Maya. "We don't want the tour spread out all over the place. While each community selects the artists to be included

through an informal, juried process, artists are on the tour until they decide to end their involvement." The tour is in such great demand by artists wishing to be included that there's a waiting list for participation.

One key to creating positive experiences for the art seekers is the production of a detailed, easy-to-follow map in the Fall Art Tour brochure, so that getting lost between artists' studios is less likely. As the popularity of the tour grew, so did the attractiveness of this premier marketing tool. "We've gone from a simple brochure about the event to a glossy, four-color brochure that's much more inviting," says Maya. "Because of all the competition, we have to keep the Fall Art Tour fresh and keep people coming back for something new." Besides a dynamic and artistically engaging website, the organization added guest artists—that may be on the tour for only one year—and GPS (Global Positioning System) coordinates for the location of each studio or gallery on the tour for visitors wishing to use this feature while driving from artist to artist.

The Fall Art Tour has also netted dividends to area businesses since many of the thousands of art seekers travel from larger cities and areas throughout the Midwest. From no-vacancy signs posted at area accommodations to bustling restaurants and other gift or antique stores, the Fall Art Tour stimulates tourism in these communities. "The tour is a wonderful introduction to our communities," shares Diana. "People have positive experiences during the tour and come back again at other times of the year."

"The tour has become a pivotal part of many artists' livelihoods," notes Diana, regarding the increased impact of the event on her family's bottom line. "It's something Tom and I start preparing for in August in order to have a good selection of pottery available. As well as we can be prepared, that's how well we'll do," she says.

Artistic visions seem to come easy to many of the artists associated with the tour, some of whom have quite a talent for turning dreams into artistic renditions of reality—and the good life. "Who knows," jokes Maya, trying to mask her sense of earnestness, "maybe the entire state will become one big art tour every fall, when the leaves start turning." Until then, the artists on the Fall Art Tour will be busy at work creating one-of-kind pieces and one-of-kind experiences for those who walk through the doors of their studios and galleries.

INNOVATIVE FARMING

Wisconsin is known for its strong and diverse agricultural traditions. Picturesque dairy farms, abundant fields of corn, rolling pastures and lush forests create the idyllic landscape that residents and visitors treasure.

Delve more deeply into today's agricultural landscape and you will find a wealth of farm ventures that push beyond the established models of row crop, dairy and livestock farming. In this chapter we meet people who have taken farming to the next level—through innovation, hard work and a commitment to working in concert with natural systems. They include farmers who invite people out to share in the joy of the farming experience, who develop long-lasting relationships with their customers, and who believe strongly that the food they produce should be of the highest quality and reflect the integrity of the land and the farmers that are its stewards.

From apples to vegetables, from chickens to trout, the stories featured here are a sample of the revolution taking place across the state—a revolution that makes Wisconsin a leader in sustainable and organic agriculture. This is farming where quality trumps quantity and where success is measured against a triple bottom line that accounts for financial, environmental and social considerations.

SWEET ORGANIC PASTURED PROFITS

Krusen Grass Farm, Elkhorn

With 120 dairy cows, 25 steers and a flock of about 100 chickens using an intensively managed rotational grazing system, the Krusen Grass Farm has emerged as the Midwest's leading example of how sustainable agriculture can be profitable, ecologically sound and provide an enviable quality of life for the farm's owners and their three children. Since 1990, Altfrid and Susan Krusenbaum have managed their 320-acre farm organically—guided by the biodynamic philosophy that considers the entire farm as a living organism—to produce organic milk, beef and eggs. Their farm, located outside of Elkhorn, has been certified organic since 2002.

A postcard perfect farmstead, Krusen Grass Farm's tidy nature radiates the deeply-rooted devotion to stewardship that the Krusenbaums share for the land. Altfrid and Susan rent their land on a long-term lease from Yggdrasil, a nonprofit land trust organization that owns the land. This land rental blends long-term stewardship with the economic viability of farming, a win-win for both the land trust and the farmer, harvesting a stable quality of life for the Krusenbaums.

"The first investment should be in your cattle," says Altfrid, his warm German accent revealing his European roots. "Cattle

appreciate in value as they get older, multiply and regenerate. The second investment should be in your equipment," he adds, with a confident wink in his eye. "We rent just about everything else including our house and land. We can rent our land cheaper than if we were to buy it, when you add in interest payments, insurance and property taxes. We wouldn't get a good return on our investment until we sell it."

The big money for the Krusen Grass Farm has always been in its high quality, certified organic milk, sold to Organic Valley Family of Farms since 2002 and earning a net farm income of about $1,000 per dairy cow or $120,000 annually. "Milk is what counts the most," shares Susan, in response to its role in their operations. But diversification also plays an important part, since the pastured chickens rotated through the fields after the cows are valuable for eating the fly larvae that hatch on the cow manure. Accounting for about 10 percent of Krusen Grass Farm's gross receipts, the grass-fed beef from steers bred, born and raised in the pasture is directly marketed to customers who pick up their order at a nearby meat processor.

Deeply committed to organic agriculture from the start, the Krusenbaums farmed organically in the early 1990s when no organic pricing premium existed. "I think because we farmed organically back when no profit motive existed, we've earned credibility within the sustainable agriculture movement today," Susan comments. Respect and interest for Krusen Grass Farm's approach to agriculture brings hundreds of people from across the globe to tour the operation. "Education and tours remain important to us and something we always take the time to do as our way of extending the movement."

Experimentation characterizes Krusen Grass Farm. Reducing labor costs on the farm led Altfrid and Susan to explore rotational grazing for the dairy herd, allowing them to shave off $3 per hundredweight

in production costs. "That's where it all began, to reduce labor costs," says Altfrid. "We started with the advantage that we didn't come from traditional farming backgrounds," he admits. "I didn't have a farming father looking over my shoulder telling me what I should or shouldn't do. We were freer than other people who take over the farm from their parents. In that sense, we were able to try new things."

The Krusenbaums don't fear failure, but rather embrace it as a learning experience. A past attempt at organizing a cheesemaking cooperative led to new marketing experience. "Our cheese cooperative experience will pave the way for other marketing initiatives," says Altfrid.

The Krusen Grass Farm fosters experimentation in other ways, too. In addition to help from their children and a part-time mechanic, one or two interns work on the farm each year, gaining hands-on training. "Our interns graduate when they're left alone on the farm while we're away," laughs Altfrid.

To encourage the development of their interns, Krusen Grass Farm has adopted a more progressive and egalitarian approach to ownership of the operations: dairy share-milking. A step up from internship, share-milkers garner not only experience but also share the profits from milk sales. When they leave they are also vested with a share of the heifer calf crop born during their training. The share-milker makes a commitment to stay on the farm, usually for three years. The share-milking apprenticeship provides a tangible venue for Altfrid and Susan to leave a legacy of fostering the next generation of farmers. Says Altfrid, "Our goal is to incubate and develop a career path for young people to get started in farming and to turn share-milking into a viable career."

"We look to New Zealand for inspiration," says Altfrid. "In the New Zealand society, dairying is among the most sought after occupations. It provides a desirable way of life." Besides providing the idea kernel for share-milking, a visit to New Zealand led Altfrid to acquire a 16-unit, swing-over milking parlor and adopt a seasonal approach to dairying whereby the cows are allowed to dry up and stop producing milk for a few months in the late winter. Large sows are kept on the

farm, not for meat, but to root through the manure left over from the over-wintered cows, turning the manure into compost—yet another innovation employed by the family.

"In New Zealand, 95 percent of the dairy farms are seasonal and pasture based," explains Altfrid. "By operating seasonally, we can now have a life and I can go on vacation with my family." This approach not only keeps cows healthy, respecting their natural cycles, it gifts the Krusenbaums with a break from the dairying routine and encourages off-farm travel. In contrast, most conventional U.S. dairy farms, regardless of size or scale, leave no option for owners to get away from their operations for more than an afternoon between milkings. Altfrid uses the winter months, when the cows dry up, to consult and speak on pasture-based dairy operations, helping others learn from his experiences while adding another diversified source of family income.

"If it's not good for me, why should it be good for the soil or the animals," asks Altfrid rhetorically, regarding their commitment to using no antibiotics, hormones or chemicals in their operations. "Our organic and biodynamic approach to grass farming and dairy production is no more labor intensive than non-organic approaches," he says, dispelling the myth that going organic is more labor intensive. "There is one exception," he continues with a smile, "cutting the grasses and weeds under the electric fences."

But such a long-term dedication to the land, farming and the animals reaches beyond labor costs and profits for the Krusenbaums. As Altfrid and Susan share breakfast with their two sons and daughter after morning chores, frothy and fresh milk alongside conversation grace the table. If the cows at Krusen Grass Farm ever need a reminder of the fertile good life they have, they need gaze no further than alongside their barnyard, beautified with a rainbow of petunia boxes.

"EAT MY FISH"
Bullfrog Fish Farm, Menomonie

Herby Radmann's Bullfrog Fish Farm was born, he says, "out of the gumption and wit of rural culture and the cool, clean, sweet waters of the Chippewa Valley." His famous smoked trout spread is heavenly. Scoop some onto a cracker and taste the smell of a distant bonfire on a cool night, gently blended with the delicate flavor of wiggling fresh rainbow trout.

That glorious spread is just one of numerous aquatically-themed offerings from the farm, where value-added marketing has expanded the product palette to encompass everything from a catch-your-own entertainment destination to delivered specialty cuts and fish farm memorabilia designed by local artists. Located in rolling farm country a half-hour south of Menomonie, the Bullfrog Fish Farm lounges in a green valley at the end of a winding gravel road. Around the last bend the funky buildings and placid pond come into sight. There's a row of kids and adults along the shore, with lines in the water. The farm crew is smiling. The visitor begins to appreciate that this whole Bullfrog thing is about way, way more than fish.

"Soul Proprietor" Herby, much appreciated by friends and customers for having the wit of a stand-up comedian and the mind of a philosopher, explains that this venture has much to do with a mission of preserving rural ways of life. "Our model is the family farm," he says. Economics, though necessary, are secondary.

Growing up with his family's market vegetable farm on the rural outskirts of St. Paul, Herby explains, "I picked up the lifestyle, where work, play and social times are often indistinguishable." But grandpa's home place became a McDonald's and the field is a strip mall, and as a young adult Herby moved on to other pursuits. Yet he and his wife, Vicki, never lost their dream of country life, and in 1973 they initiated their five-year plan to find a rural home.

In 1978, according to plan, the Radmanns bought 100 acres in Dunn County with the help of a group of like-minded families and established the "Bullfrog Spring Community." "We moved 80 miles to come home," Herby says. But the plan didn't cover learning how to live once they got to the country. "As we learned new ways, I sometimes thought our first job here was to provide humor to the neighbors."

A year later the Radmanns bought additional adjacent land. "The idea was to build a rural business. But we couldn't think of one," says Herby. "We needed $1,000 a month to live, so I had to come up with ten $100-a-month ideas." These ranged from painting, selling eggs and picking up garbage to child advocacy and marriage counseling. The land was just a place to live until 1987, when Herby realized their sandy field sat only eight feet above the nearby Chippewa and Red Cedar Rivers. A hired bulldozer quickly hit clear, clean water, and the vision of a fish farm was born. After seven more years of planning and building as it became affordable, Bullfrog Fish Farm opened for business.

From the start, the high-quality products and Herby's genuine affection for people of every shape and size has aided the development of local sales and made the farm a favored destination. These days Bullfrog Fish Farm produces 15 to 20 thousand pounds of rainbow trout each year, sold to an array of restaurants, retail outlets and farm visitors. It provides four full-time jobs during the season and regularly hosts tour groups ranging from family reunions and buses of retired folks to food science students from the University of Wisconsin-Stout and state agricultural officials researching value-added agriculture. The farm brings a regular flow of fishing tourists to the area and has also become a local cultural

mecca, with occasional live music, frequent bonfires and strong support for local artists. "Art helps us see what we've got and why it's worth saving," Herby says.

Herby has also provided local and state political leadership along with a few innovative ideas for keeping family farmers in business. He's been prominent in the Wisconsin Aquaculture Association and has helped change state laws to increase opportunities for fish farmers. He's gone from searching for ways to make a living on the land to educating others about the economic possibilities of value-added agriculture and agritourism. In 2004, Herby's neighbors voted him the "Dunn County Outstanding Farmer of The Year."

Buttons advertising the farm are available in a wonderful array of designs, the work of Rick the drum maker and artist-of-all-media who created the famous fish spice blend that is now sold separately to interested cooks. Rick was one of the original hobo chefs. "When Rick would hobo he would play the pots and pans between orders," Herby laughs. "Hobo chefin'," by the way, developed during the farm's construction phase when, after long days on the job, the crew cooked up meals of "low expectations and big surprises." Now it's another value-added and popular feature, offered on weekends to visitors anxious to eat their catch.

The farm's purpose, ambitions and ambience are adroitly captured by Herby's proud claim to be the founder of "The Preservation of Rural Character Society." Asked for a definition of rural character, he replies, with a characteristically gentle smile, "Like other matters of the heart, it's best to be left undefined."

Though Herby's mustache, long braid of hair and "Eat My Fish" bumper stickers have become familiar parts of the local scene, none of this recognition came easily. And there are still miles to go to

retirement and the next generation. "My crew is making a living, I'm making an investment," he says, adding that his wife continues to work off the farm. "When you pick meaning and purpose, sometimes you sacrifice economics. We're still playing it day to day. You've got to have faith."

Growing into a regional, more financially viable provider of fish and fun has been a tough nut to crack. In 2005, Herby "took a sabbatical" from politics to focus on figuring out how to find long-term economic sustainability. He thinks there are three reasons the enterprise has struggled: being underfinanced from the start; the demise of rural service providers and workers; and a system that offers no paths for small producers into mainstream food distribution. Typically, he's addressing these issues in an innovative fashion. He's offering farm shares to outside investors to finance needed expansion, work-to-own options for employees and a concentrated effort to develop regional distribution for fish farm products.

The larger goal is to help preserve small-scale farming as an economic option and way of life. "Not everybody's going to grow up and become a part of corporate America," Herby pauses. "The family farm can be a place for them." He's looking at the long-term picture as well, realizing that it takes time to establish a name and a business. "I'm old enough now that I'm thinking generationally," he says. Even if he's never able to quit worrying about the economic wolf at the door, the next generation should have the established reputation and product distribution network to be comfortable.

After all, though the money is necessary, it isn't the gist of the matter. "This farm has a million successes, a lot of memories, and if it weren't for money I'd be a rich man," Herby smiles. "I've done a lot of things. I am this."

ACRES OF APPLES AND MORE
TURKEY RIDGE ORGANIC APPLE ORCHARD, GAYS MILLS

From the livestock grazing between the apple trees to the canned apple pie filling on the shelves of the on-farm store, diversification refrains throughout Turkey Ridge Organic Apple Orchard's business philosophy. Based in the rugged countryside outside Gays Mills and built on a core commitment to organic apple growing, Turkey Ridge is an inspiring example of innovation in agriculture—redefining and reinventing itself with each growing season.

From the first apple tree plantings in the late 1980s, Turkey Ridge started as an organic operation. The original founder, Richard Gainor, wanted to plant and run a certified organic apple orchard from the start, focusing on disease-resistant varieties of apples. Over the following 20 years the farm underwent a variety of evolutions with the realization of the labor intensity and manpower needed to run an organic orchard, which led to the formation of the worker-owned Midwest Organic Fruit Growers Cooperative in December 2003. Today, a core shareholder group manages Turkey Ridge with various helping hands and supporters.

"A worker-owned cooperative is one of a few viable options for large-scale organic fruit growers in the Midwest, given that it is a full-time job for one person to manage about 1,000 trees, yielding around 3,000 bushels," comments Alex Person. Alex is one of the three core shareholders along with Faye Rogers and Greg Welsh, all of whom live in the farmhouse on the property.

Turkey Ridge encompasses 289 total acres, with about 75 orchard acres containing 8,000 apple trees. The remaining acres are in woods, pasture and growing fields. "We focus on growing 22 disease-resistant apple varietals that will mature at different points during the growing season," Alex explains. "William's Pride matures first at the end of July and Enterprise needs a frost to ripen around mid-October." Other disease-resistant varieties in the orchard include Priscilla, Prima and Freedom.

The co-op's underlying commitment to organic apple growing fuels the manual labor needed to run such an operation. "Growing organic apples is a labor-intensive challenge," says Alex. "In midsummer, for example, half of the green apples need to be removed to increase the size of the final apples, otherwise all the apples would be very small. Conventional orchards use various sprays to get half the apples to fall off; however, we thin the trees by hand and we also hand-harvest."

From fungus to bug invasions, different problems arise throughout the year that require different pest management strategies. "There really isn't one right way to run an organic orchard, as these pests vary tremendously geographically," notes Alex. Turkey Ridge aims to manage the farm holistically, innovating ways to manage pests and processes to both improve soil fertility and diversify the business.

One new pest management strategy Turkey Ridge has introduced is rotationally grazing five pigs, nine sheep and 1,200 chickens. The animals are moved to a new half-acre plot every three to four days. "The chickens pick up bugs and the pigs eat grubs, till up the soil and add manure," shares Alex. "The sheep eat the windfall apples that fall to the ground, which is a very important part of orchard management and our farm plan. Every apple that falls needs to be removed, as various bugs invade these apples and become pest sources for the next growing season." Constantly moving the animals is a key element of this strategy. If they are left too long in one spot, the sheep would start chewing the trees and the pigs would root up young trees. At the end of the season, some livestock are kept for breeding and the rest processed for meat sales and the co-op members' own use.

The bulk of Turkey Ridge's apples go into cider and cider vinegar, both of which the facility is licensed to process on-site. Products are primarily sold wholesale to loyal food cooperative customers in Wisconsin and Minnesota. Additionally, apples are processed at a local commercial kitchen facility into jellies, apple syrup and the co-op's newest value-added ventures: apple pie filling and frozen apple pies. An expanding customer base continues to grow retail sales through the on-farm store at Turkey Ridge that is open seasonally from August until early November. This means workers don't need to spend time away from the farm at farmers' markets, with customers making annual apple pilgrimages from places such as Chicago, Duluth and Iowa.

Other diversification efforts include a pick-your-own squash and pumpkin patch and cord firewood during the fall season. "We planted a couple acres in asparagus, raspberries and strawberries that will enable us to open earlier," notes Alex. "We've also started supplying morel mushrooms, that grow up under the apple trees in spring, to Organic Valley Family of Farms."

Wreaths made from curly willow and harvests of the herb echinacea are also in the farm diversification plan. "We've found it much easier to make a thousand dollars here and a thousand there than trying to make all our money from just the apples," Alex explains.

Balancing a manageable workload while sustaining a profit remains an ongoing challenge for Turkey Ridge. Alex, Faye and Greg cut back their production load this past year to ensure they could deliver on orders. Greg also works for Organic Valley and Alex takes on a variety of jobs during the off-season including long-haul trucking. Still, apples remain the core passion of Turkey Ridge. "I think I touched every apple in some capacity before it left the farm this season," says Alex with a smile.

CROSS-CULTURAL FARMING
THE STRENN FARM, GREENLEAF

As you travel over the rim of the magnificent Niagara Escarpment and begin the descent into the historic Fox River Valley, the century-old Strenn farm lies before you like a treasured patchwork quilt. During midsummer the quilt is made up of numerous shades of green. But as the season progresses, it appears as if the farm is being viewed through a kaleidoscope. The once prominent greens change hues, and yellows and browns begin to seep into the picture.

Upon closer examination, other colors begin to appear. Ripening Thai hot peppers add brilliant pinpoints of red, orange and purple to the landscape. The maturing winter squash add shades of blue, salmon, orange and dark green to the mix. There are thousands of these squash throughout the fields—raised primarily for their stems and blossoms, not the squash itself. While seasonal changes have always been a part of farming, on this farm change over the years has been particularly significant.

The 81 acre Strenn farm is located in southern Brown County, just north of Greenleaf. Over the years, Brown County has been home to numerous dairy farms, cheese factories and related businesses. However, as residential construction expands, more and more farmland disappears each year. In 1970, Brown County had 1,950 farms covering over 277,000 acres. By 1999, the amount of agricultural land had decreased to 213,000 acres with fewer than 1,275 farms.

The farm first entered the Strenn family in 1913 when Henry and Inez Strenn purchased the property from the Hocker family. Henry worked the land with a team of horses and raised dairy cows, hay

and corn. Henry and Inez's son, Donald, who was a millwright at a local mill, purchased the farm in 1947.

Much to the dismay of his father, Donald retired the horses and bought a tractor. He had to hide the tractor at first since he knew his father would not approve of this drastic change. While Henry never approved of the change, it was one aspect of "modernization" he had to accept. Donald continued to milk cows, cut hay and raise grain on the 42 tillable acres. He also made cabinets for local clients during the winter months. In 1959 Donald's brother, Howard, and his family also moved to the farm. Howard was

employed at a local factory but raised a few chickens, ducks and horses in his spare time.

In 1969, a major fire destroyed the dairy barn and Donald decided that he would retire from the dairy business and devote all of his time to cabinet making. The land was then leased to local farmers. Later, when Donald's health declined, Howard took over the farm and continued to raise chickens, ducks, horses and a few cows. However, the bulk of the tillable land was rented to local farmers for hay and grain.

The Catholic Diocese of Green Bay contacted Howard in 1989 to see whether he had land available for a Hmong family to use for raising vegetables. The Diocese had been assisting Hmong immigrants who had relocated to the Green Bay area. The Hmong people, who lived in the mountains of Laos, had assisted the U.S. military in Laos during the Vietnam War and were later persecuted by the Communist government after the war. Thousands of Hmong fled Laos to refugee camps in Thailand and were later relocated to the United States by the U.S. government.

Howard agreed to lease the family one acre of land to grow vegetables. The arrangement worked well, so he invited the family back the following year. The Hmong family returned to lease land each year, not only raising vegetables for their family but eventually selling vegetables at the farmers' markets in Green Bay and De Pere. The family members saved their money and eventually were able to purchase their own land east of Green Bay in 2005.

Since that time, many other members of the Hmong community have leased parcels from Howard, and more recently from his son Ed, who took over the farm in 1998. Like his father, Ed continued to have positive experiences working with the Hmong growers and in 2006 he expanded the vegetable rental area to 16 acres.

Ed's involvement with the growers doesn't end with the signing of the lease. He also prepares the land in the spring and plows under the vegetation in the fall. He works with the Hmong growers during the summer and, if necessary, will plow an area in July or August so that a fall crop can be planted. Even though communication can sometimes be difficult, due to the varied English skills of the growers, through his ongoing involvement Ed has gained a great respect for the Hmong who farm on his property. Ed says, "These are the nicest people to work with. I watched Dad do it and I have been fascinated with people who physically touch the soil. The camaraderie of having people here on the farm is a godsend and no other culture is as polite. These are just super, hardworking people."

Pha Soung, of Green Bay, talks about how she values Ed's support. Pha and her husband have been renting land from Ed for seven years. Along with their 15 children, whose ages range from 7 to 26, they are planting, weeding and harvesting over four acres of vegetables and flowers this year. They sell their flowers and vegetables on Saturday mornings at the Green Bay Farmers' Market. Pha and her husband were full-time farmers in Laos, growing primarily squash and beans. Everything in Laos was done by hand and they used slash and burn techniques. "Here," Pha notes, "Ed helps plow." The only other modern equipment used by Pha and her husband is a small rototiller and a walk-behind seeder. All other work is done by hand. When asked why they choose to farm, Pha explains, "When the weather is nice we like to go outside and that is what we did in Laos."

Pha and her husband are one of over 20 families currently renting land from Ed. When asked what he has learned through his experience, Ed says, "Respect for other cultures. And that it is still possible to have a close family and work the land: I've seen children and grandparents work side by side in the field. The grandparents set the examples of quality of work and the children respect their elders."

Both the Strenn Farm and the land surrounding it have seen many changes over the last 100 years. However, in many ways this farm has come full circle. Just like in the days of Henry Strenn, the land is being cultivated using minimal equipment by people who feel they have a close connection with the land and enjoy seeing the results of their labors. The partnership between Ed Strenn and the numerous families growing crops on his land should guarantee that this piece of property will not succumb to the blight of urban expansion and will be kept in agriculture for many years to come.

THIRD GENERATION POTATO FARMING

IGL FARMS, ANTIGO

Entering the cavernous wood-walled storage bins at the Igl Family Farm feels as though you're moving into an ancient world. The cool, dark rooms are mounded full of earth-perfumed potatoes of many types and colors. Aromas of garlic, cloves and peppermint waft from the processing room, adding a surprising complexity to the sensual experience. Here in the potato storage building of the Igl Farm one begins to appreciate the elemental nature of potato farming in Wisconsin.

Brian Igl and his younger brother Brad represent the third generation of Igls farming on this 200 acres of land outside of Antigo in north central Wisconsin. The two brothers farm with their father, Tom, but are not exactly following in the footsteps of their forebears.

The primary difference from the previous generation of farmers is that the Igls now farm organically. They have been selling certified organic crops, including potatoes, oats and peas, since 1997. With 63 acres of organic potatoes in 2006, the Igls are the largest organic potato producers in the state. "In 1995, I came back from college, didn't think I'd stay in farming, but got intrigued with organic and we decided to try it," Brian says. He had heard stories of organic farmers making money, and with the conventional potato market being very poor at the time, the family decided in 1997 to convert 20 acres to organic production. "I never liked handling chemicals," Brian adds. "We've been really happy with the change to organic." The change to organic production is the reason for wafting scents of garlic, mint and cloves in the air. These essences are used to ward

off bugs and strengthen potato plants so they can better resist disease. "Organic production is all about learning new things," Brian notes. "We are constantly trying out new ideas." The packing shed's ambiance certainly benefits from these new ideas as well.

Converting to organic production has expanded the farm's diversification. Organic systems require crop rotation and recommend cover crops to increase fertility. For example, the Igls will plant potatoes in a field one year, and the next year plant field peas. In the third year the field will be planted into oats, then a clover/grass mix, and then the rotation will start over again with potatoes. This rotation of crops is important for organic management for several reasons. Varying the crops means pest and disease cycles are interrupted. There's not much food in an oat field for potato beetles! Each crop will also add to or use up different nutrients in the soil. Legumes such as clover or peas will add back nitrogen into the soil that is used up by the potatoes.

Brian's curiosity has led him to be one of the first producers of organic field pea seed in the Midwest. "I switched to field peas when I found it hard to get non-genetically modified soybeans," Brian says. He prefers to not use genetically modified products, which aren't allowed in organic production according to the National Organic Standards. Brian has been very happy with the field peas, and uses them on the farm to feed chickens, hogs and beef cows. He uses registered foundation seed so that he can then sell the peas as certified organic seed to other producers.

One of the challenges of diversified crop production, however, is the added burden of using or marketing numerous crops. Although the focus of the Igls' attention is on finding markets for their organic potatoes, they also sell organic oats and peas. Finding and keeping markets for this wide variety of crops takes a lot of time and attention. As the primary marketing manager for the farm, Brian's outgoing personality has served him well in seeking new and expanded markets for the farm's bounty.

The family has participated in several groundbreaking programs, such as a University of Wisconsin "College Food Project" that brings Wisconsin farm products into its dining hall service, and the developing "Wisconsin Homegrown Lunch" program that plans to offer Wisconsin produce in school lunches for grades K-12. The Igls participate in the "FamilyFarmed.org" project, which connects consumers to local farmers in the Midwest. Brian's family has also worked with several local and regional retailers to develop Wisconsin-based markets for Igl potatoes, including food cooperatives and locally owned grocery chains. "My ultimate goal is to sell every potato within 300 miles of the farm," Brian notes. "I really believe in local food systems—where the consumer can know the farmer. Large-scale commodity distribution isn't a logical use of resources."

At this time, however, a majority of the Igls' organic potatoes get sold into the commodity market. Around the Midwest and as far

away as Philadelphia, customers can pick up "Igl Farms Organic Spuddies" in eye-catching red, brown or yellow plastic bags, each with its own "potato spuddy" mascot designed by Tom Igl. A picture of the family, a paragraph on the Igls' commitment to growing healthful, high-quality food and a tasty recipe all grace the back of the bag.

Besides potatoes, seeds and feed, the Igls also produce pasture-raised beef, chickens and, occasionally, pork. Neighbors benefit as well. "We raise it for ourselves so it's easy to raise a little extra for neighbors who like good meat," Brian says. He likes to experiment with different feed rations, and this year is raising his young broilers on a mix of peas, oats and triticale.

All the men enjoy fieldwork, but each has his specialty. Tom is the primary machine operator, Brian acts as field scout and does the farm's marketing and Brad keeps the books and is the farm engineer. After working at the John Deere Corporation as an engineer for several years, Brad decided to return to farming with his family in May 2005. Everyone is glad to have both Brian and Brad back home on the farm, even more so since the boys' mother, Nancy, died suddenly of a heart attack in November 2005. "She was our rock, the center of the family," Brian sighs. The men of the family are still adjusting to all the implications of their loss.

The family has never been high profile. In fact, Brian says that their organic potato production may be "one of the best kept secrets in the area." But, most of the neighbors know the Igls are organic farmers. The Igls have hosted field days offering information about their successes and challenges to others interested in organic potato production. In addition, Brian has presented at regional conferences on organic production practices and his family's successful marketing techniques. "We've had lots of visitors on the farm, even some recently from central Europe," Brian claims. "It's great to share with farmers and researchers from other places."

"Each year we learn how to be better organic farmers," Brian concludes. "Except for our personal challenges last year, it was a really good farming year. We continue to improve our soil, managing minerals and the soil life, so we can sustain production year after year. That is what sustainability is all about—leaving a legacy to the next generations."

Stepping back into that filled cavern of potatoes, one is drawn into the timelessness that the earthy smells and sustainably produced food represent. The Igl Farm certainly feels like a place that will continue to do a good job of sustaining future generations.

FARMING AS IF EVERYTHING MATTERS

Good Earth Farms, Marshfield

From the soil on his farm to his customers' doorsteps, everything involved in producing and marketing Good Earth Farms' organic beef, pork, lamb and poultry is important to founder Mike Hansen. Which means this is not, by any stretch, conventional modern farming where the goal is simply to raise the largest possible crop. This type of farming is better understood as systems management, the meshing of the many interconnected parts into a life where everyone wins, from the earthworms to the kids to the chefs who feature Good Earth Farms' organic, pasture-raised meats on their menus.

"Our goal is to prove a system of agriculture that is sustainable environmentally, financially and socially—and socially is the family," Mike says. "You look at the whole, the environment you're in, and you're not the master—you work with the cycles that are here, the seasons. You don't fight them. It's the way God intended this to occur, so that's the way we do it, and our customers are the people who appreciate and respect that, and look forward to being a part of it."

In terms of a working day, this means that Mike spends as much time working with customers as he does at actual farming, and that kids and family time are always a priority. This summer that's been a struggle, with his wife, Deb, having to put in considerable overtime at her off-farm job, while Mike and the three kids, Ben, Jake and Mariah, dealt with a drought and a rapidly growing business.

"We struggle to get time for vacations, to go fishing. The reality of 15 and16 hour days has really hit this summer. But it's not as bad as it sounds. I'm here with the kids. It doesn't matter if you're working or you're fishing, time with them is time with them. And it gets better every year," Mike says.

Since the Hansens moved to 80 windswept acres southeast of Marshfield in 1995, they've been gradually growing their operation until it now includes eight member farms and customers from Maine to California. In 2006, the group produced 11,000 chickens, 2,100 turkeys, 34 hogs, 20 lambs and 30 head of beef, all raised organically and on pasture. Good Earth Farms' products are available in select stores and restaurants in Wisconsin and Illinois, as well as directly from the farm's website to individual customers. Specialty products such as chicken hot dogs, nitrate-free ham and bacon and beef soup bones are available as well.

"The most important aspect of this farming operation is the marketing," Mike explains. "If the marketing wasn't there, what we're doing couldn't exist. We have the volume to make retail stores happy. Except for beef, we rarely run out of things, and we have a variety of products available. We cater to folks who care about what's in their food." Good Earth Farms also has, as a specific part of its mission, a commitment to keeping prices affordable.

The member farms, primarily Amish and also certified organic, joined over the past few years, after Mike's marketing success created more demand than could be supplied by one farm. "Our poultry processor, Wapsie Produce in Decorah, Iowa, got us together," he says. "I needed someone to produce the way we were, and they needed someone to market. We put together a grower's manual and fine-tuned it with the group's help. It's working very nicely, and we've become very good friends. We're growing and changing this business to flow with what works best. Right now we're limiting it to ten farms. If we find that markets far exceed what we can produce, I'd rather franchise this concept (than add more farms). People want to buy from the farm—they want to talk to the farmers who produce their food."

Anyone who buys from Good Earth Farms is welcome to call or visit and ask questions. One of the first things a visitor might notice is the richness and diversity of life—both domestic and wild—on the farm. Those windswept acres are windswept no more, and the million-gallon manure pit is long gone.

"When we moved here, the farm was sick," Mike says. "There were just a couple viable trees up by the house, and the cows had basically destroyed the 15-acre waterway. We've planted around 15,000 trees, the waterways have been restored, and we've got two wildlife ponds. Now you can't see the house from the road."

The backbone of the farm system is permanent pastures that are never plowed. "I strongly believe that grazing is what helps the soil the best. Our soil profiles when we do our testing just keep getting

better. The only tilled soil is where the pigs were—it looks like a bomb went off," Mike smiles.

Pigs are by nature rooters and diggers, and allowing animals to behave naturally is the rule at Good Earth Farms. Mike simply drags a field cultivator behind his tractor to smooth pig-plowed ground. He rotates the Belted Galloway cattle through a series of fenced pastures that grow a salad bar of grasses, clovers and forbs. The breed was chosen, he says, for its ability to perform well on grass, its heavy hair coat that withstands Wisconsin winters effortlessly and for the white around the middle which gives them their nickname of "oreo cookie cows"—which adds a little style to the farm scene. They are never fed grain, an unnatural food for a ruminant with a four-chambered stomach. Since grass-finished beef cooks quicker and at lower temperatures than grain-finished beef, and since the whole food system matters and not just the farm, customers receive cooking instructions with their beef.

The poultry, housed in movable, floorless coops with free access to pasture, do what poultry love to do: catch bugs, peck at greens and seeds, scratch and dust themselves in the dirt. If birds can look happy, these are happy birds. But for the first time this year, there's no poultry at the Hansen farm. All the birds are being raised by other members. "If I was going to do the marketing and the shipping, something had to give," Mike says. "I miss the turkeys. Their curiosity and mannerisms are endearing."

"Animal welfare is the top of the list for us," he adds. "If you treat these animals with respect and give them the living conditions and food they're supposed to eat, their health and stress issues disappear. This manner of taking care of animals makes you feel good. If you think of this as holistic, you can't treat them any other way."

Wapsie Produce owner Mark Nichols, who handles all poultry processing for Good Earth Farms, believes Mike is a very unusual farmer. "Not only is he articulate and honest and smart, he's not afraid to work and get his hands dirty," says Mark. "Many farmers raise their crops *to* market, Mike thinks about raising them *for* a market. He's trying to raise good stuff, not lots of stuff. He's organized and balances his business with family time. He takes his boys fishing!"

Mike believes this kind of farming is good not only for everyone and everything around him, but for himself as well. "I think I finally found the perfect job for the attention deficit person."

BUILDING COMMUNITY

The word "community" brings to mind many images—from communities of place that are tied to specific locations to communities that form around shared interests. Communities come in all shapes and sizes—some tight-knit and full of traditions, others loose and informal. What all communities have in common is a connectedness among people.

With a focus on connecting community members through powerful commonalities, the stories shared here bring people together around a diversity of focal points. We see how community can spring up around a farmers' market; how reintroducing traditional foods, like bison and white corn, can help strengthen Native communities; how the airwaves can be used to not only entertain but to build bridges across cultural divides; and how communities can come together to fulfill their dreams.

Sometimes community just happens. Other times it happens because of the hard work and diligence of those who nurture and build community connections. The following pages provide just a few glimpses into the importance and power of community in rural Wisconsin.

PROSPERITY AND PUBLIC LIFE
DANE COUNTY FARMERS' MARKET, MADISON

A foggy Saturday morning dawns in late August and the vendors have arrived on the square. As they unload produce from pickup trucks and vans and set up their tents and tables, it begins to look like a carnival or a country revival. And, in many ways, it is both. Among the nearly 200 farmers' markets throughout the state, Wisconsin's largest market, the Dane County Farmers' Market in Madison, has become a favorite destination for residents and visitors.

The Dane County Farmers' Market has been "the" place to be on Saturday mornings since it was established by a 1972 partnership between the city of Madison, the Dane County Extension Office and the Central Madison Committee of the Chamber of Commerce. It is the largest producer-only farmers' market in the country, with all displayed farm products grown or produced in Wisconsin.

Every Saturday from late April to early November, rain or shine, the stands of over 150 vendors surround the State Capitol Square. There are 300 vendors in the outdoor market's membership. In the winter, the market goes indoors to a location nearby. In a testament to the market's commercial success and good management, there is a three-year waiting list for new vendors. Nonprofit and political groups set up booths on the capitol grounds, while arts vendors and musicians position themselves across the street. A smaller market takes place every Wednesday just off the square.

The Dane County Farmers' Market offers an uncommonly full range of vegetables, fruits and organic produce. You will find a wide array of cheeses, fresh fish, eggs and meats, including beef, pork, poultry, lamb, bison, venison and rabbit. There are flowers and plants, baked goods and specialty goods like honey, preserves, maple syrup, pesto and more. In early summer you will find asparagus and morel mushrooms. As summer warms broccoli, lettuce and strawberries, then beans, tomatoes, melons, sweet corn and potatoes will appear. Fall brings beets, cabbage, kohlrabi, apples and much more.

Shoppers begin strolling around the square before the sun's rays have topped the downtown buildings. Vendors are busy arranging their wares—a tableau of bright zinnias, a sculpture of peppers in shades of red, orange, purple and yellow, rows of preserves in jars that pick up the morning light like prisms.

For early shoppers, the slow stir of the walk around the square marks an easy beginning to their weekend. These are people taking their time, letting their senses wake up to the colors and smells of the market, rubbing sleep from their eyes as strains of a fiddle rise across the street. When you ask them what makes this market so special, they say the variety, the sociability and getting to meet the growers.

Market regulars Kathy and Larry Dickerson, of Sun Prairie, say they are drawn by the overwhelming visual feast of colors, shapes and textures of the food and flowers, and they enjoy the people. They anticipate running into old friends. Kathy describes the market as "a slow antidote to the busy work week."

BUILDING COMMUNITY

57

It is a pleasant surprise to find so many people simply taking their time at the market. Joining the crowd is like stepping into a biosphere of harmony and prosperity. For a time, the turmoil of the world does not intrude on the business of finding the perfect box of cherries or a fresh-baked loaf of bread.

By 9 a.m. the sidewalks are full. People perch on the steps and benches of the capitol grounds. Kids play. A string band kicks off a tune. The energy rises as the crowd moves counterclockwise around the square—people are relaxed and smiling, enjoying fresh brewed coffee and good company. It's a morning outing made special by the possibility of seeing a familiar face.

Urban sociologist Ray Oldenburg calls public markets a "third place." In contrast to the first place (home) and second place (work), third places are public places, such as markets, coffeehouses and cafes, where people gather and interact. Such places nurture a community's social life and foster social equality. Jane Jacobs, a writer and advocate of "livable cities," said "Sidewalk contacts are the small change from which a city's wealth of public life may grow." That wealth is shared generously at a farmers' market. From a multitude of small transactions—roma tomatoes from this vendor, cloves of garlic from another—come the makings of a thousand healthy meals and new relationships between consumers and growers.

Soon it seems everyone is bearing sacks bulging with produce, as kids trundle by with balloon animals and half-eaten apples. Shoppers continue to look, picking the one box of raspberries they favor over all the others. Calls of "hot, spicy cheese bread," "How may I help you this morning?" and "How have you been?" mingle with children's happy

shouts, the sounds of traffic and construction and, over it all, the rich tones of a bagpipe.

The morning is anything but slow for the vendors, who are in constant motion, making sales and fielding questions about the varieties of produce and sharing recipes and cooking tips. They fill produce bags, make change and restock as supplies dwindle.

Tricia Bross, of Luna Circle Farm, is an organic producer and operator of a community supported agriculture program, or CSA, where members pay at the beginning of summer for a weekly box of produce.

"Working with the CSA is a one-way transaction," says Tricia. "Putting food in boxes, I may not even meet the members or talk with them, so it's not a social activity. I love the market. And this market has a good return, with so many people. Today's a good day."

As the morning passes, the crowd takes on a more determined gait. Early shoppers give way to those who fear they may have missed out on something, as drum beats echo across the square. Couples and families are scattered on the grassy lawn; parents resting, people tasting something they have just purchased.

"People like this market," Tricia says. "People like to see the ingredients and interact with growers. They like to know where their food is coming from. And, they like to support local farmers. When you say agriculture in Wisconsin, that means local, direct marketing."

While public markets contribute to rural economic growth and benefit local businesses, they also provide a source of nutritious foods and help communities address issues of hunger and food security. Wisconsin's farmers' markets participate in the WIC (Women, Infants, and Children) Farmers' Market Nutrition Program and the Seniors Farmers' Market Program, providing vouchers to low-income families and seniors to help pay for fresh produce.

Farmers' markets showcase the farmers, entrepreneurs, artists, activists and educators who participate, bringing rural and urban citizens together in new ways. Consider the impact of all this activity on market day, as it rewards the growers and those who shop. How many Wisconsin kitchens will hum with the labor of preparing fresh vegetables, meats, cheeses and herbs, and fill with the aroma of a delicious meal? Friends and family will gather around the table, a sunny bouquet of flowers at the center, to share the meal, extending the sphere of harmony and prosperity deep into each home.

COMMUNITY THROUGH FRESH FOOD
Vermont Valley Community Farm, Blue Mounds

Part homecoming, part celebration of harvest bounty, part merry fun. The clock strikes 9 a.m. on a misty early September Saturday morning as members of Vermont Valley Community Farm pile out of their cars and frolic down the path to the rows of overflowing ripe tomatoes. Farmer Barb Perkins welcomes everyone with energetic enthusiasm to this southwest Wisconsin farm's annual tomato U-pick for CSA (community supported agriculture), warmly greeting both the long-time shareholders and new members as if they were family. CSAs sell shares of the farm's bounty in advance of the growing season and provide regular boxes of fresh produce to shareholders. "This is our first year as CSA members and first time to the farm," shares a twenty-something couple, as Barb orients them to picking rows while her husband, David, checks in the rest of the arrivals. From families with toddlers in tow to young couples and seniors, all have picking bags and baskets in hand. "You can pick 15 pounds of tomatoes, take as many cherry tomatoes as you like since they're starting to split and help yourself to basil," explains Barb, her members appreciatively smiling as if they just won the local organic flavor lottery.

Located 30 miles west of Madison in a fertile green valley of Vermont Township, Vermont Valley Community Farm provides more than certified organic food deliveries to members. The farm serves as a tangible connection point to build community through fresh, seasonal food access, while providing profitable income and a high quality of life for the Perkins family. While David grew up on a Wisconsin farm, both he and Barb's income came from office jobs until 1992, when they became members of one of the first CSAs in Madison. "That first CSA experience brought us to this farm," explains David. "Philosophically, the CSA philosophy resonated with us and made such logical sense, from upfront payment to making direct connections between members and the farm." Adds Barb, "'We can do this' was our motivational refrain, and we started looking for property a short drive from Madison."

In 1994, the Perkins launched their first CSA growing season with 50 CSA shares. "Only one of those first 50 shares came from someone we didn't already know," laughs Barb. "We tapped into our friends for our first share members as they knew us, trusted us and wanted to support this new venture." Today, Vermont Valley Community Farm feeds around 1,150 people from 25 cultivated acres, offering over 150 different produce varietals and a menu of member CSA package options, from spring greenhouse shares to storage vegetable shares. Vermont Valley's core market focus is the CSA. While selling relatively small amounts to Willy Street Co-op and Whole Foods Market in Madison, Vermont Valley chooses to not sell at farmers' markets, focusing instead on CSA supporters.

Barb and David prioritize on-farm experiences for members, a philosophy that has deepened member dedication to Vermont Valley while providing the Perkins with a social means of connecting with their shareholders. "Members come out here for a U-pick or event and leave with such appreciation for their experience," adds Barb. "That means a lot to us."

Annual farm event traditions have evolved over the years, often sparked by farm abundance. "The Pesto Fest started during a year when we were overflowing with basil. It's the event highlight of the summer, bringing over 100 people out to the farm each September." These larger events, including a spring pea pick, July corn boil and October pumpkin pick, provide a marketable advantage for people to choose a Vermont Valley Community Farm subscription. Over the years, the Perkins learned that creating events around hands-on activities provided a more enriching experience for everyone. "We started hosting a typical spring open house and gave farm tours," Barb explains. "Then there was a bumper pea crop so we invited everyone out to pick peas, providing a much more memorable, hands-on experience."

Interestingly, the more the on-farm events grew, the more Barb and David learned to keep things simple. For the potlucks during the pesto fest and corn boil, the Perkins used to set up dozens of tables and water jugs with cups to accommodate the over 200 attendees. "This created a lot of work and stress for us so we asked folks to bring their own dishware, drinks and a picnic blanket and to carry home their own waste," adds Barb. "Folks were more than happy to do this and by doing a bit more they became more active and involved with the event, and we were able to enjoy things more as well."

The Pesto Fest ranks high on the community-building scale, as members harvest basil together and then whip up and share their pesto creations on-site, bringing along their own food processors and other ingredients. "We learned to set out a tray and ask everyone to leave us a sample of their pesto so we could make sure we get to try everything," chuckles David. Vermont Valley members love their pesto and every season everyone receives their own basil plant. "We found this to be both added value for members while keeping things a lot simpler for us because basil is extremely difficult to keep fresh after harvest. By teaching folks to grow their own, we don't have to worry about delivering basil."

Thanks to these on-farm experiences, blended with the overflowing, high-quality share boxes, members of Vermont Valley Community Farm deeply support their CSA. So much so that people want to

support the farm even after they've left the area or their kids have fledged and they don't need as much weekly produce. The Perkins came up with a "Food To Share" program to address such situations, whereby individuals "join" Vermont Valley by contributing $100 to cover low-income family shares. "'Food To Share' is a great value because you still can come to all the on-farm events," Barb explains. Over $4,500 was raised for the program this year, resulting in share memberships for over 30 families, administered through the Madison Area Community Supported Agriculture Coalition "Partner Shares" program.

Other members keep connected to Vermont Valley through the worker share program. Over 50 members sign on as "worker shares" for the season, committing four hours per week to work on the farm. This program cost-effectively provides a significant chunk of Vermont Valley's staffing and, again, increases members' dedication to the farm. Surprisingly, most of the worker share participants are motivated not by the economic side of receiving a free share, but rather the fulfillment—and fun—of hands-on farm experiences.

Supporting other fledgling farm-based enterprises forms a core philosophy of the Perkins. They help other businesses promote their products through Vermont Valley's share base, providing the opportunity for members to purchase flower, egg and cheese shares from other local farmers. "We know we're very particular about high quality product, so we've learned to partner with farmers

we've known for a long time, in some cases former employees who've gone on to start their own business," comments Barb.

In a new diversification effort, David now grows and sells certified organic seed potatoes. Despite the fact that Wisconsin ranks high in potato growing volume, no local source for organic seed potatoes existed. "I thought to myself, this is silly that we have to order our potatoes from places like Maine or Washington. Somebody needs to raise organic seed potatoes in Wisconsin, so I guess it has to be me," smiles David. Abiding by both stringent federal organic and state seed potato standards, David plants five acres in potatoes, about one third for the CSA harvest, one third for store sales and the other third for seeds, which he then sells to over 50 area farmers.

Barb and David welcome their 25-year-old son, Jesse, in his recent choice to join the family farm business, and look to increasing share volume and profit in the future to support him as well. "This property was originally a family farm, but had been divided and sold off by the time we came along in the early 1990s," David comments. "We're proud that it's a vibrant, healthy diversified family farm business again," he adds, waving goodbye to a blissfully content member with overflowing bags of tomatoes and basil in tow.

THE KERNEL OF ONEIDA CULTURE
TSYUNHEHKWA CENTER, ONEIDA

At the Oneida Indian Nation of Wisconsin, just west of Green Bay, the farms will appear similar to others in the state, down to the red barns, dairy cows and fields of corn. But if you stop for a minute and shuck some of the corn, grown in both large and small plots, you will find gleaming kernels of white flint corn.

The Oneida, who call themselves Onyota, brought the corn with them in their migration from New York State in the 1820s. Traditionally, white flint corn was grown by many Oneida families and was seen as central to the survival of the tribe and the community. It was not just a food source, but their Tsyunhehkwa (pronounced Joon hey-kwa) or life sustenance. Over the years, the practice of growing and eating white flint corn disappeared.

In the 1970s, Tsyunhehkwa, the Oneida Nations' community and culturally based agriculture program was started. In 1992, the tribe acquired some white flint corn seeds from the Oneida Nation in New York, and white flint corn began to be grown again. Ted Skenandore, farmer at Tsyunhehkwa, says, "The corn is from the original diet and was one of the sustainers of the Oneida. Planting the corn is a way of keeping the traditional food line going and it can help with the health of the people."

The Tsyunhehkwa Center has reintroduced organically grown foods to the Oneida people to ensure a healthier diet and lifestyle for tribal members who had long been dependent on commodity foods. By doing so, it also seeks to educate tribal members and the wider

community about Native traditional food systems, which are rooted in the ancient past and updated to the modern age with the use of environmentally sustainable technologies such as a solar-heated greenhouse. In the spring, the greenhouse offers a starter package of vegetable plants to anyone interested, for a minimal price.

The farm involves Oneida families and members of the community in every aspect of white flint corn production. The farm holds two events each year to educate both tribe members and the general public about the corn. In late summer, when the corn is at the "milk" stage, the farm holds its Green Corn Festival. At this time some of the corn is harvested and a soup is prepared. In addition to the corn, the soup contains squash, beans and beef. The soup is served with a host of other dishes including roasted potatoes and wild rice with beef that has been slow roasted for 24 hours. The meal is then topped off with a choice of cherry or apple pie, with crusts that melt in your mouth.

The Husking Bee is held after the fall harvest in October and is critical to the selection of seed for the next year's crop. After husking, the white flint corn is braided, hung and dried. Throughout the year volunteers shell the corn by hand and store the kernels in bins. The bins, which are used exclusively for white corn storage, are periodically delivered to the cannery for processing.

The processing division of Tsyunhehkwa is based in the Community Cannery. This division includes education in food canning,

indigenous food workshops and food preservation assistance. The products it creates include canned white corn soup, dehydrated corn, traditional corn bread and corn flour.

At the Community Cannery the corn is first cooked with hardwood ash to break down the hard outer shell and then canned or dehydrated. The corn, canned either with or without meat, is traditionally used to make a nutritious corn soup. The dehydrated corn is either sold or ground to make corn flour. The cannery also uses the flour to make traditional corn bread. Because it has a short shelf life, the bread is baked about four times a week.

The cannery is a significant asset in the community's food system. Not only is white flint corn processed here, the facility is also used to provide workshops to community members on food canning and they can do their own home garden canning here.

The distribution division of Tsyunhehkwa is referred to as Retail and Community Services and has a retail store located just west of Green Bay. The store is open to the public and offers a wide range of products including "Herbal Harmony" tea blends and bulk herbs, traditional medicinal herbs, white corn soup, dehydrated white corn, raw white corn, corn flour, traditional cornbread, wild rice and many other items. They also provide workshops, books and pamphlets on preventative healthcare, traditional foods and herbs.

Perhaps most importantly, the traditional farm reintroduces a cycle of cooperation within the community, with Oneida and their neighbors of all generations working together to harvest, process and distribute the crops. The white flint corn and other food crops provide a cultural connection to tribal ancestors and a reason to rebuild a sense of community and nationhood.

RESTORING BISON TO THE PEOPLE

HO-CHUNK NATION, MUSCODA

For hundreds of years, American buffalo, also known as bison, roamed free across the interior of North America. Used for clothing, food, shelter and tools, bison held great meaning for many different American Indian peoples. But in the 19th century, encouraged by the federal government, white hunters devastated the bison population as part of a strategy to overcome western tribal nations. Mighty herds of bison that numbered in the tens of millions were reduced to only a few hundred, seemingly destining the bison to extinction.

But the Ho-Chunk Nation, along with more than 40 other tribes across the country, is working to reestablish healthy bison populations on tribal lands. And in the process, the Ho-Chunk hope to improve the health of their tribal members by reconnecting with the diet of their ancestors.

Bison Prairie 1 is the Ho-Chunk Nation's 640-acre ranch dedicated to the reintroduction of the bison. Begun in 1996 and comprised of ancestral land along the Wisconsin River near Muscoda, in Richland County, the site also contains several effigy mounds on its wide, flat vistas. The Ho-Chunk see their continued ownership of the land as necessary to ensure the long-term protection of the mounds from development.

The Ho-Chunk people once inhabited several million acres of land extending throughout southern Wisconsin and northern Illinois. Abundant wildlife, including wolves, bison, moose, bear and elk, surrounded their villages. As the line of European settlement moved increasingly westward, however, the Ho-Chunk were forcibly removed from their traditional land by the United States government and the land was given to settlers. Although now confined to a smaller area of the state, the Ho-Chunk Nation is dedicated to protecting, restoring and improving the natural resources on their land.

Because of the high rates of diabetes and heart disease among tribal members, and because of the reported benefits of bison meat, tribal leaders decided to develop a bison herd on their Muscoda property. They joined the InterTribal Bison Cooperative, a nonprofit based in Rapid City, South Dakota that helps to coordinate and assist tribes in the reestablishment of bison herds. The Ho-Chunk Nation acquired their first four bison—one male and three females—from Yellowstone National Park. An outbreak of brucellosis led the park service to make healthy bison available to Indian Nations for purchase as an alternative to killing them to prevent the spread of disease.

Today, the herd of 152 animals is managed by a crew of four and overseen by Larry Garvin, executive director of heritage preservation for the Ho-Chunk Nation. The bison are grass-fed and rotated through ten separate pastures, drink water from a rain-filled ravine and seldom receive medicine. Bison meat is served at traditional feasts organized by the Tribal Aging Unit, an agency that provides services to older residents and to individuals under doctors' care for certain illnesses.

"The long-term impact on the community is significant," says Larry. "Such healthy meat can help combat diabetes and certain heart diseases." Bison meat is both lean and nutritionally dense. And it appears to taste good, too. A survey of elders who had eaten bison from the ranch reported a 90 percent approval rate. But this has created a problem as well.

So great is the demand by tribal members that it has outgrown the capacity of the Muscoda farm to supply enough bison meat. The InterTribal Bison Cooperative currently supplements the Ho-Chunk Nation's supply. Distribution is determined by a four-level priority system, ranging from first priority going to those with a medical condition and fourth priority being Ho-Chunk family and cultural activities.

"Acquiring enough land to maintain a self-sustaining herd without overgrazing is the greatest challenge facing the project," explains Larry. Bison require a minimum of four acres of land per animal to sustain a healthy breeding environment. The Ho-Chunk would like to obtain a contiguous piece of land that would allow for herd expansion. This would also allow them to sell meat to the general public as a means of economic diversification. But providing enough food to tribal members remains the top concern.

The bison do more than just supply food to the Ho-Chunk, though. Bison provide a cultural connection and symbolic base of strength and unity for the Ho-Chunk people, providing a daily reminder of the role the animal once played in their history—a history that tribal elders want to ensure is passed on through their children.

In addition to bison, the Ho-Chunk have restored nearly 100 acres of land at the ranch to natural prairie. They have also established a watershed management plan with the Natural Resources Conservation Service and the Wisconsin Department of Natural Resources to address erosion control along the banks of the lower Wisconsin River. Other measures have been taken to maintain wildlife habitats, such as leaving certain fields fallow and eliminating fencing to allow for the free movement of wildlife.

Besides their land in Muscoda, the Ho-Chunk Nation is involved in a jointly owned and managed nature reserve at the site of the former La Farge Dam in Vernon County. The Kickapoo Valley Reserve covers 8,500 acres and is a cooperative effort between the state of Wisconsin through the Kickapoo Reserve Management Board and the Ho-Chunk Nation. The Ho-Chunk are also involved in negotiations with the state, local communities and conservation groups to acquire a portion of the land at the former Badger Army Ammunition Plant in Sauk Prairie, with the intent of reintroducing bison and restoring prairie grasses.

Bison Prairie 1 is operated as an "open farm" to encourage greater environmental protection and education. Tours are given nearly year round, allowing visitors to enjoy the scenery and feed the bison while learning about agricultural practices in the context of Ho-Chunk culture. The Ho-Chunk Youth Department has also made the farm its permanent home for the Summer Youth Conference, allowing kids the opportunity to take part in the ranch.

"Providing opportunities for tribal members to see the herd whenever possible and to participate in the annual bison round-up is the biggest reward," says Larry. "And hopefully we can improve the health of our people at the same time."

MUSIC IN THE PARK

LUCIUS WOODS PERFORMING ARTS CENTER, SOLON SPRINGS

Solon Springs is clearly a "little town that could"—and did. The impending construction of the Highway 53 bypass rallied its residents to take action in 1992, and by the time the new highway was dedicated in 1999, they had certainly done so. Imagine an open air amphitheater and grand concert shell made out of local red pine and tamarack and framed by towering pines, with Upper St. Croix Lake as a backdrop. Now imagine summer performances by the Duluth Superior Symphony Orchestra or Cajun, Irish or acoustic bands. Welcome to the Lucius Woods Performing Arts Center.

A series of community meetings in 1992, attended by 10 percent of the local population, were used to identify goals that would benefit the community. One of these was to make better use of Lucius Woods—a 40-acre parcel named after Nicholas and Emma Lucius, who had helped preserve it in the early 1900s. The Solon Springs Development Commission, a group created as a result of these meetings, took the lead on realizing the community's goals—including developing Lucius Woods into a performing arts venue.

Although this is a story of volunteerism and broad-based community support, Mary and Frank Giesen are closely identified as leaders in the realization and success of the performing arts center. Frank and Mary worked together tirelessly on this project. As Frank puts it, "I was the sit 'em down guy and Mary was the cook—but the reason people came was because she was a good cook." (After Mary's death in early 2005, the concert shell was dedicated as the Giesen Concert Shell in honor of both Frank and Mary.)

There were many pieces to put into place and a lot of people to "cook" for. The Lucius family had originally sold the park land to the state as a reserve, but it eventually became the property of Douglas County. "Putting a music festival in a park was controversial," says Frank. The county wanted to preserve the integrity of the park and had questions about how to safely put on events for large crowds of people. Fond du Lac had a similar facility, so a community group spent a day-and-a-half there

BUILDING COMMUNITY

learning the ins and outs of creating a performance venue and holding events.

While the community hired an acoustical consultant from the Twin Cities and an architect with experience with log structures, the rest of the undertaking was homegrown. The logs came from Douglas County forests—and loggers donated their time and equipment to bring them to the site. Wisconsin Conservation Corps crews and inmates from the Gordon Correctional Center peeled the logs. All electrical fixtures were donated and a sign in a union hall yielded volunteer electricians who wired the facility on weekends. In the end, a finished facility worth $300,000 was built with $80,000 of county funding. The Lucius Woods Performing Arts Center, an acoustically excellent log structure set in the woods of northwest Wisconsin, opened for its first season in 1994.

Each season brings a new line-up of performers who entertain and inspire. But over the years, two constants have emerged: the Duluth Superior Symphony Orchestra and the Whitesidewalls. The orchestra has been intimately involved since the beginning and uses Lucius Woods as its "summer home." The Whitesidewalls emerged as a crowd favorite during the second season and have since become a program fixture with sponsorship provided by an area business. Frank says, "The Performing Arts Center brings a type of entertainment and culture to Douglas County that never existed before."

Frank knows that the benefits are not just cultural, but also economic advancement. Dean Amhaus, former director of the Wisconsin Arts Board, dramatized the economics of a concert on a small rural community by showing pictures of people queued up at the Solon Springs' Dairy Queen before and after concerts. Barb DeFore, office manager of the Solon Springs branch of the National Bank of Commerce, notes that bank deposits jump on concert weekends, with people being drawn in for the day or the weekend.

Barb, like many others in the community, has been involved with the Performing Arts Center since the beginning. She was on the original board of directors and helped form the "Friends of Lucius Woods," a volunteer support group that raises money and helps with the concerts. Barb emphasizes, "The reason Lucius Woods has done as well as it has is the volunteers dedicated to it." She also sums up the community's sense that it "wants the town to grow while keeping a small town feel in mind."

A "typical" concert is a picture of a community in motion. High school students, in what has become a tradition, put up the fence, set up chairs in the amphitheatre and do the tear down at the end of the concert. The Volunteer Fire Department handles traffic direction and parking. The Friends of Lucius Woods cover ticket duties at the gates as well as sell Lucius Woods merchandise. The area Lions Club is the on-site food and beverage vendor. People from near and far park their cars and walk through the woods to the amphitheatre—or take the shuttle bus. The seating capacity of 2,000 means that the population of the community quadruples when the performance is a popular one and the weather is favorable.

The reach of the concert series has grown over time. For years, Frank has taken brochures all over northwestern Wisconsin. He tells of the earlier years when some locations in Hayward, for example, were not interested in the brochures because they wanted people to spend time and money in their community. "Now," he says, "they ask for the brochures and say 'you have something we don't have.'" Similarly, tourist venues in the Cable area have told Frank, "thank god we've got another place to send people."

In May 2002, Pat Pluntz became the center's first full-time general manager. Surrounded by donated equipment and furnishings in an office provided at the bank for a fraction of its rent value, Pat says, "The community is just so generous ... the broader community believes in what we do here. And it is not just the volunteers, but local businesses as well. They are willing to help in any way. This community takes very strong ownership of this venture."

The mission of the performing art center is "quality professional entertainment." Symphony performances in a rural park would certainly qualify. The overwhelming support and involvement of the Solon Springs community has clearly shown and continues to show what is possible when a community believes anything is possible.

NORTHWOODS COMMUNITY RADIO
WOJB, LAC COURTE OREILLES BAND OF THE LAKE SUPERIOR OJIBWE, HAYWARD

Where in Wisconsin can you hear big band tunes in the morning, Native American news at noon and honky-tonk as the evening stars appear? Only in the listening radius of WOJB radio, 88.9 on the FM dial, "Listener Supported Community Radio in the Northwoods of Wisconsin." While a short year ago those listening to this eclectic mix would have lived within a 120-mile radius of the station headquarters in Hayward, with the addition of "WOJB Live" web streaming, listeners now tune in to this diverse programming from as far afield as Germany and Japan.

WOJB is broadcast from the Lac Courte Oreilles (lak coot o-ray) Indian Reservation, home of the Lac Courte Oreilles Band of the Lake Superior Ojibwe. The station first hit the airwaves in 1982 with a very specific mission—to connect the voices and activities of the Native people with the surrounding non-Native community.

The political climate in the Northwoods was very tense in the 1970s and 80s. Native tribes and residents of surrounding communities were polarized over issues such as the reinforcement of treaty rights and the strengthening of tribal sovereign governments. Savvy tribal leaders recognized that a lack of understanding of Native cultures among the non-Indian population was fueling the tension. WOJB was born out of this tension, as a way to maintain a peaceful environment in northern Wisconsin by increasing communication between the cultures. "Not only are we here to preserve, protect and promote Native culture," says station manager Lori Taguma, "but we are an important source of local news and information for the Northwoods community."

Broadcasting with 100,000 watts, the station is one of the strongest principal Native radio stations in the U.S. and the only one east of the Mississippi River. It is organized as a nonprofit corporation, licensed to the tribe but supported financially by the community. "Forty percent of our operating funds come from listener members," Lori notes. "We have members that have been with us since the beginning and continue to support us year after year." Other funding comes from the Corporation for Public Broadcasting and community underwriters.

Although overseen by the Lac Courte Oreilles tribal council, the station is truly a product of its community. The majority of the eight full-time and two part-time employees are tribal members, and 35 volunteers contribute programming from throughout the region. "We are a voice for the community—every day hosts interview Lac Courte Oreilles members and others about services and activities in the area," Lori notes. Local programs range from the popular "Local Morning Edition" with host Eric Schubring during "drive time" (8 to 9 a.m.) to "On the Porch" and "In the Garage," local music and interviews in the afternoons, and a wide array of local music programs after the dinner hour. Regular topics of interest include local and regional politics, organic gardening tips, environmental issues, local health offerings, community support programs and much more.

"People are always stopping by to chat" Lori says. "WOJB is where native and non-native people mix." Lori also notes that the station has played an important role in bringing the various tribes

BUILDING COMMUNITY

of northern Wisconsin, and the U.S., together. Members of the other Native tribes in Wisconsin are frequent guests on interview shows, and WOJB plays nationally syndicated programming from American Indian Radio such as "Native American Calling" and "National Native News." Seventy percent of the programming is locally produced, with the remainder syndicated national or regional programs.

The national programs are an important source of news and information. The programs from American Indian Radio highlight national Native issues and keep the Lac Courte Oreilles tribal members up to date on stories from sister tribes across the U.S. Other national programs, such as "Democracy Now" with Amy Goodman, "This American Life" from WEBZ in Chicago and "As It Happens" from the Canadian Broadcast Service are well regarded for their hard-hitting commentary and journalistic integrity. "Our news programming and eclectic music collection are appreciated by tribal members as well as the local community," Lori adds. Even folks traveling through, or those with summer homes in the area, have commented on the quality of the programming and miss it when they are out of the station's reach. The new web-streaming service will help computer-savvy travelers and seasonal residents keep the station tuned in year-round.

WOJB listeners rely on the station to not only inform them about upcoming events in the community, but the station is also frequently "on the road" with staff, broadcasting from a local powwow or hosting the annual Hand Drum contest. The "Events List" on the website details activities as diverse as child play-group parties and library book readings to polka festivals, tribal meetings and environmental information events. Announcements of community events are made during station programming throughout the day, allowing listeners to stay abreast of a wide diversity of area activities.

Plans for the future include programming that will take advantage of the new potentials created though web-based podcasting. One new initiative involves more programming in the native Ojibwe language, with archives available for podcast. There is a movement at Lac Courte Oreilles to teach young and old alike the native language. Programming offered in Ojibwe strengthens learning possibilities and keeps the language alive for Lac Courte Oreilles residents and those interested around the U.S. and beyond.

WOJB is a cosponsor, with the Lac Courte Oreilles Tribal Historic Preservation Office, the Lac Courte Oreilles Ojibwe Community College Cultural Resource Center and the Lac Courte Oreilles Ojibwe Community College Native American Studies Department, on an oral history project entitled: "Nibabaa-asiginaamin dibaajimowinan: Gathering Stories from Lac Courte Oreilles Tribal Elders and Community Members." This two-year project, just being completed, records cultural interviews from tribal elders and community members. These will soon be available via podcast, allowing people from all over the U.S. and the world to listen and better understand the Lac Courte Oreilles culture. There are plans to expand this project to record stories of daily lives, in both the native language and English.

The WOJB "listening family" is strong and diverse. Acting as the voice of the Northwoods community, it is clear that this special radio station is much more than a place to tune in on the FM dial. WOJB is not only actively achieving its mission of connecting the voices and activities of the Native people with the surrounding non-Native community, but it is also a well-regarded community treasure.

Tune in soon at 88.9 FM or at www.wojb.org. Listeners will certainly learn something about the Native tribes in the state, and enjoy a wide diversity of unique programming too.

TOWARD A HEALTHY PLANET

The natural world defines the heart of the countryside. From the northern pine forests to the oceanic beauty of the Lake Superior and Michigan shores, Wisconsin harbors extraordinary natural beauty.

In this chapter, we visit those who have made it their mission to preserve, protect and carefully utilize the gifts of our natural world. We learn how the Menominee people sustain, while utilizing, the bounty of their forest, and have done so for hundreds of years. We discover how reassembling disturbed natural environments can be the heart of a successful business. We learn how a college walks its talk by integrating sustainability in many of its operation. We meet a farm couple who have developed a holistic system that works with nature to cultivate and provide fruits for the surrounding community. Finally, we visit an innovative company that utilizes the forces of nature to feed our energy needs.

These stories highlight those who have found ways to not only respect and appreciate nature, but to harness its bounty—sustainably. They are forging partnerships with nature while sustaining themselves, their families, their communities and, in some cases, their culture.

THE ETERNAL FOREST
MENOMINEE TRIBAL ENTERPRISES, KESHENA

If you can imagine a pallet four feet wide by eight feet long, stacked with all of the timber harvested in the Menominee forest since 1854, the stack would reach a height equal to 994 miles—the distance from Milwaukee to New Orleans! In forestry terms, that's 2.25 billion board feet. Yet the Menominee forest today has more standing timber than it did in 1854. This is not a chance occurrence, or a fluke of nature, but the result of over 150 years of careful management.

"Using the natural world while simultaneously caring for its long-term sustainability is deeply embedded in the Menominee people's culture," explains Marshall Pecore. "But what many people don't know is the long history of entrepreneurship that has impacted and continues to affect the health and well-being of the tribe."

As a child, Marshall spent a great deal of time in the Menominee forest and at the local sawmill where his father worked. After attending college at Michigan Tech, he returned to become the forest manager for Menominee Tribal Enterprises, the primary business arm of the tribe. Menominee Tribal Enterprises operates and manages the tribe's business assets including forest management, logging and the marketing, manufacturing, selling and distribution of its timber and forest products.

Located in northeastern Wisconsin, the Menominee reservation is communally owned by the tribe and consists of 235,000 acres of land, of which 220,000 acres make up the Menominee forest. Because of its tremendous size, the forest can be spotted in satellite photos taken from 10,000 miles above the earth. A closer look will reveal 33 tree species including white pine, hemlock, maple, red oak, basswood and yellow birch. Bear, bobcat and a host of other wildlife make their homes here and eagles soar above the towering trees.

The land within the reservation accounts for roughly 3 percent of the Menominee people's original territory. The lands they occupied were taken over by the U.S. government through a series of unscrupulous treaties in the 1800s. But while many Indian tribes fell victim to the General Allotment Act of 1887—a U.S. policy that divided and allotted their land into privately owned parcels and undermined cultural norms—the Menominee were able to resist against it. The result is that while much Indian-owned land was lost and denuded, the Menominee were able to keep their land base intact.

This intact land base, along with thoughtful and far-sighted decisions by tribal leaders, has resulted in the Menominee forest being one of the best managed in the country. Marshall explains, "The Menominee leaders have always taken the view that the timber resource in the forest should never be harvested at a rate faster than it can be replaced." This view and the subsequent management plans have resulted in a forest that has 400 million more board feet of harvest-quality timber today than it did when it was first inventoried back in 1854—1.3 billion then, 1.7 billion now.

TOWARD A HEALTHY PLANET

Oral histories convey an early vision for forest management that was extraordinarily effective. They say, "Start with the rising sun, and work toward the setting sun, but take only the mature trees, the sick trees, and the trees that have fallen. When you reach the end of the reservation, turn and cut from the setting sun to the rising sun and the trees will last forever."

Today the management plan is a bit more complex, incorporating the latest science and technology to ensure forest and ecosystem health, yet the principles are fundamentally the same—a testament to the knowledge and wisdom of those early leaders. The Menominee forest is divided in 109 distinct compartments and managed on a 15-year cutting cycle. The type of trees in an area determines which harvest method is utilized.

In an average year the forest supplies 15 to 18 million board feet of saw logs and 80,000 cords of pulpwood. Once removed from the forest, harvested trees are taken to the Menominee-owned sawmill. Here logs are cut into lumber or molding, kiln-dried and then sold by Menominee Tribal Enterprises' marketing and sales staff.

Marshall explains, "Unlike many forestry operations, the Menominee mill sets its goals based on what the forest can sustainably deliver. If the forestry department says it's going to bring in more sugar maple, the marketing and sales department turns around and sells that." This is in contrast to many operations that let market demand determine what is cut, thus putting short-term economic gain ahead of long-term forest health. "This way we'll always have this forest for future generations," says Marshall.

These unique operating principles require Menominee Tribal Enterprises' marketing department to be both innovative and diligent to maintain profitability. They have done this by building long-term relationships with customers, negotiating annual pricing contracts and providing a quality product. This strategy, along with patience with the ups and downs of the market, has made the operation economically successful.

This success translates into over 450 jobs—making Menominee Tribal Enterprises the largest employer in the community. About 200 of these people work in the forest, 200 in the mill, and the rest in sales, marketing and administrative positions. People from all over the world come and visit to see how the operation works and how it can be a model for forests and communities in other parts of the world.

Marshall says, "What we do here is important in terms of economics and ecological health, but it is also very important to sustaining the Menominee culture. For generations the Menominee people have had a deep connection with this forest." Marshall and others at Menominee Tribal Enterprises are now working with the Menominee Tribal College to train young people who can then take leadership positions in managing the forest and running other aspects of operation.

The Menominee tribe has been tenacious in keeping the forest intact and healthy. It has not always been easy. In the 1800s, greedy pine barons threatened their vision. In the mid-1900s, a corrupt U.S. policy terminated the Menominee's status as a tribe and took away all their assets and rights for over a decade. (This policy was later overturned.) And, of course, there are often internal disagreements on how the forest and mill should be managed.

Marshall says, "Because the forest is literally in everybody's back yard, everybody feels ownership—which has its benefits, and problems." He adds, "Fortunately, people do feel obligated to follow the course that other leaders in the past have set." And because of this the Menominee forest, and the Menominee people, are in a good position as they move into the future.

GREEN TECHNOLOGY ON CAMPUS

NORTHLAND COLLEGE, ASHLAND

Wind towers and solar panels flank the buildings and grassy native plantings fringe the lawns. An electric maintenance vehicle motors silently across campus without gasoline, while 300 gallons of food scraps are churning into compost for the community garden.

Is this Sweden? Holland? Heaven? No, it's Northland College, located in Ashland, on the southern shore of Lake Superior. As part of its mission, Northland integrates environmental consciousness with its liberal arts curriculum, making it one of the select few such colleges in the country. Founded in 1892, Northland is a four-year private environmental liberal arts college with about 700 students. With one teacher for every 13 students, the relationship is personal and on a first-name basis.

Northland students come from 38 states and three other countries, attracted especially by the environmental focus. Just one mile from the lake on Chequamegon Bay, Northland College is surrounded by nearly a million acres of the Chequamegon National Forest.

Given its mission, it is not surprising that the college sees alternative energy projects as important educational tools. But with this commitment comes risk: environmental innovations can be problematic, and often require a specialist to fly in and fix them if they break. And they do break.

"In some ways we are making trouble for ourselves," says senior Ryan Nicholson, energy conservation coordinator with the college's Lifestyle & Energy Awareness Program (LEAP). "But there is a difference between Northland College and a typical business owner.... Northland is concerned with building up individuals to make a better world," he says. "The local utility company says the energy grid will never go down, but if we just bought energy from them and said, 'We don't want to install renewable energy systems because they don't make economic sense,' then no one would learn."

But Northland is a business, too. Last summer, when employees working in the new Ponzio Campus Center were fainting, vomiting and leaving work early due to heat exhaustion, President Karen Halbersleben had to consider an air-conditioning system that would make environmental and economic sense. A study conducted by Northland's director of sustainability, Kim Bro, compared a conventional system costing only $125,000 to an energy-efficient geothermal system at $330,000. But through analysis of electricity

savings, Kim found a savings of $1.5 million over 30 years if Northland were to invest in the geothermal.

"The easy decision would have been to just plunk in a regular air-conditioning unit, but we wanted to make a longer-term investment that was not only good for the College but for the environment as well." Karen says. While the system provided effective air conditioning at the outset, the college had to modify the existing heating system to best use the geothermal system in winter.

Completely hidden underground and silent, the system was installed in about two and a half months. "Without flashy symbols, there's nothing to engage people to get them to ask more questions," says Ryan, when explaining the other efficient but less visible energy-saving "work-horses," such as the boosted insulation, heat recovery system and variable-speed blower motors.

Other low-key, sustainable features on campus are SmartWood doors, windows and furniture; low-flow toilets, showerheads and faucets; glue-lam support beams (sheets of wood glued together to create a big beam instead of one big old tree trunk); linoleum flooring—made by a low-impact process combining sawdust and linseed oil—in kitchens instead of petrochemical-based vinyl; and low-VOC (volatile organic compound) paints and carpet glues that do not give off toxic fumes.

"They are not high-profile items," says Ryan. "That's why we put in other features like the solar hot water heaters, photovoltaic panels and the wind tower. No one gets inspired by low-VOC paint except the painter."

The 17-kilowatt wind turbine installed alongside the Environmental Living and Learning Center (ELLC) dorm in 1997 was a maintenance nightmare. "It was very sensitive, and thus difficult to keep running because of lightning strikes and power surges," says Erik Guenard, manager of campus facilities. Only recently replaced due to constant urging by students, the new one is only 10 kilowatt, but more reliable. "It's running like a top," he says. The wind turbine and photovoltaic panels combined at maximum capacity only produce 5 to 7 percent of the energy for the

Environmental Living and Learning Center, but Karen understands the significance of the wind tower as a symbol for all things environmental and listened to the students' objections when it was out of order after every lightning storm. "They thought it was hypocritical for Northland to leave it broken for months and months. What they didn't understand was that it was built as an experiment, so it might work, it might not. But I saw that it became a priority, because we want to be doing everything we can to walk the talk," she says. Ryan agrees, "It's there, it looks sharp, and when we see the windmill spinning, it makes us feel good."

Northland College keeps learning lessons from embracing and tinkering with green technologies. In 2002, Northland bought the Earth Tub, an electrical composting machine capable of turning 300 gallons of food waste per semester into usable compost—in theory. "It's been through many different stages of problems," says Anna Hochhalter, one of the student compost workers. "As Maintenance fixes one thing, something else break. The current issue is warping—the cover warps with changing temperatures, so it takes two people to rotate it when it used to only take one."

Every day Anna collects approximately 30 gallons of compostable material from the cafeteria. That turns into 600 gallons a year of fertile compost for the Mino Aki community garden on campus. Though troubled by its use of electricity for a process that doesn't naturally need it, Anna understands why Northland bought the machine. "A pile system could work, but it would take a lot more human interaction and devotion. The Earth Tub isn't working perfectly, but it's working."

A student-initiated Sustainability Charter passed in 1998 added another level to the environmental mission: "We believe our greatest legacy, both to ourselves and to the outside world, is to change the way we think about living, learning and doing business. As Northland College moves into the 21st century, the best of our ideals as an environmental liberal arts college can be channeled into long-term efforts to sustain living communities," states the charter.

"But it's like a marriage," says Kim. "We've made the commitment, we've celebrated our vows, to have and to hold and all that stuff..., but now who's going to do the laundry? We're trying to do something different and you can't take any step in the process for granted."

Nature-Inspired Landscape Solutions

Applied Ecological Services, Brodhead

Since its humble beginnings in 1975 processing prairie seed in an old dairy barn, Applied Ecological Services (AES) has blossomed into a diversified company, carrying on its commitment to science-based ecological restoration and land stewardship. Founder and owner Steve Apfelbaum began this endeavor as a way of putting into practice Aldo Leopold's "land ethic." Today, more than 100 highly-trained ecologists, botanists, wetland scientists, landscape architects, planners, engineers and others focus on ecological consulting and restoration design services, environmental permitting services, contracting services and managing nurseries that provide seed and plant materials for over 700 projects annually.

With annual revenues in excess of $12 million, AES leads the nation in the restoration of native prairies, wetlands, savannas,

woodlands, lakeshores and stream corridors. Earning widespread accolades for their nature-inspired solutions to some of the most troubled and ecologically degraded places on Earth, AES consistently proves that what's good for the environment also saves money and improves the quality of life for all of a community's residents—including the flora and fauna.

AES makes winning international design competitions seem easy. But it's AES's broad base of international experience, solid depth of knowledge of regional issues and multidisciplinary consulting team that makes the company a good fit for their equally diverse clients—which include federal, state and local governments and agencies, foundations, colleges, religious organizations and corporations. AES has restoration nurseries in Minnesota and Kansas and offices in Wisconsin, Illinois, Kansas, Minnesota, New Jersey and Pennsylvania.

The redevelopment of the Hank Aaron Trail in Milwaukee's Menominee River Valley is one example of their work. One section of the river was lined with rail yards, landfills, brickyards and steel pylons. AES looked at the situation and developed a plan that would use nature as an investment tool for the redevelopment. "Our team took a place that was no place for people or nature and turned it into 1,200 acres of urban renewal," beams Steve, who could easily don the title of Father Nature. "Now the brownfields have transformed into parks for recreation, habitat for fish and birds and restored wetlands for storm water management. We have helped naturalize that stretch of river, reconnecting it to flood plains and creating a nature-inspired plan for flood water management."

This Milwaukee project is among hundreds of similar projects, most in the United States. On Petty Island—an industrial brownfield with toxic waste sites on the Delaware River in Pennsauken, New Jersey—AES implemented a four-pronged approach: restoration—bringing back healthy ecological systems;

remediation—cleaning up contaminated and toxic areas; redevelopment—integrating land development within the naturally occurring ecological context; and reclamation—stabilizing and reestablishing plant cover to disturbed areas.

"We're different than many other companies in that we're science based," says Steve, who is trained as an ecologist and is the author of the upcoming book, *Nature's Second Chance*. "We study how historical ecosystems manage rain precipitation, for example, and learn how to emulate nature to manage storm water in urban areas." He continues, "We've learned how to save developers as much as 15 to 60 percent of development costs—amounting to tens of millions of dollars on their projects. We do this by eliminating the need for underground storm sewers by using, instead, native landscapes, restored prairie, wetlands and forests." Often, the nature-inspired approach to solving problems offers a marketing opportunity to developers and regulators as well.

Another fast-growing field where AES leads is conservation development, focusing on urban residential and commercial uses of degraded agricultural or industrial lands. "Conservation development is about the consolidation of human settlement," explains Steve. "They're places where there are equal or greater numbers of people living on increasingly smaller acres." The now-famous Prairie Crossing, located in Grayslake, Illinois, is one such example. It devotes 30 percent of its 670 acres—formerly in commodity crops of corn and soybeans—to residential and commercial developments with the remaining 70 percent restored to native prairie, wetlands, woodlands and the like. Besides living in energy efficient homes, residents have access to locally grown food and renewable energy generated on site, with hundreds of acres set aside for nature's sake and recreational opportunities.

As a complement to its science-based approach to nature restoration, ecological economics predominate in AES endeavors.

"Native landscapes are less expensive to maintain than formal landscapes and lawns," explains Steve. "Maintenance of a formal lawn at a corporate headquarters in Milwaukee or Chicago can cost as much as $1,000 to $2,000 a year per acre. But maintaining that same land in a prairie and wetland costs as little as $50 to $200 per year per acre. Installing sod on a new site costs as much as $14,000 an acre whereas prairie costs $1,500 to $4,000 an acre." Prairie plantings save money for the companies, universities and municipalities willing to change their approach to landscaping. These plantings also provide recreational and ecological benefits, which include managing storm water runoff and improved water quality.

In partnership with other companies and U.S. agencies, AES helped spawn the 1993 wetland bank legislation. This legislation created the means by which wetland restoration could be consolidated into large wetland projects that would be more ecologically sustainable and viable. When wetlands are lost to a proposed construction project, companies, organizations or municipalities can buy credits through larger wetland restoration projects off-site. These off-site wetland projects tend to be more cost-effective for the developers while also more ecologically sound from the perspective of accomplishing actual ecological goals related to wildlife management and water quality.

"When we first started helping draft the wetland bank legislation in the 1980s, we found that the wetlands that developers re-established on-site as compensation for lost wetlands often ended up being little more than a detention pond for their parking lots," says Steve. After the legislation was in place, AES and Land and Water Resources, Inc. partnered to design and construct the Otter Creek Wetland Mitigation Bank in St. Charles, Illinois—the first private wetland bank in the United States—into which developers could buy credits in an off-site project. "Suddenly, the scale of the project became ecologically significant and our impacts meaningful," Steve says.

Satisfied clients lead to a never-ending list of new prospective projects for AES. "As a part of our recently completed strategic plan," says Steve, "we're positioning our company to have the capacity to take on the world's largest ecological problems. We're going to go from hundreds of acres in restoration to millions of acres. The recognition of and actual needs for such work is expanding exponentially." AES serves the critical role of mediator between human communities and natural communities enabling both to flourish.

Admits Steve, "It's about humility at all levels of what we're doing. We can't and don't claim to completely understand everything related to the economic, social, political and ecological aspects of our projects. We do, however, have open ears and a clear head to think about the future. We're rethinking how we view the landscape, trying to demonstrate how changing the way we approach restoration and conservation will outweigh the preconceptions that many hold about how the landscape is supposed to look." Applied Ecological Services is doing it one flower, pond, woodland and savanna at a time, community by community, neighborhood by neighborhood, city by city—changing hearts and minds, one person at a time.

THINKING GLOBALLY, ACTING LOCALLY

ECO-MUNICIPALITIES ON CHEQUAMEGON BAY, ASHLAND AND WASHBURN

A groundswell of interest to create an "eco-community" in the Chequamegon Bay of Lake Superior took off like wildfire in 2004.

Earlier that year, Ashland City Councilor Mary Rehwald traveled to Sweden to find out how that country had managed to create a network of 60 eco-municipalities that had initiated remarkably successful eco-projects. Mary brought back real-life tales of how one city reduced fossil fuel use by 90 percent and how another uses "life cycle analysis" as a review standard for housing developments. She also learned about the building of a retail "green zone" in northern Sweden that reduced energy consumption by 70 percent and fresh water use by 90 percent.

Mary explains her motivation for the Swedish trip: "I knew Sweden had worked on these issues for over 20 years. I wanted to go there to see what our future might look like if we were to take a similar path." Most of the communities Mary visited in Sweden had adopted the "Natural Step," a framework that is now used increasingly around the world by local governments and businesses. It follows scientific principles that go beyond political persuasions.

Describing what she discovered when she returned to northern Wisconsin, Mary says, "I knew something was afoot up here the night I walked into a local auditorium to give a slideshow on what I had learned in Sweden and there were 169 people crowding into the room. It's one of the few times in my life I felt like I was in the right place at the right time. Since that night, many of us who are

working on rural sustainability issues have pretty much found each other up here."

Following up on that first meeting in 2004, several actions in the Chequamegon Bay area have underscored local concern about global warming and the desire to do something positive. An eco-municipality resolution was brought to the Washburn City Council by Mayor Irene Blakely the summer of 2005, and its passage established Washburn as the first eco-municipality in the United States. A similar resolution was passed by the Ashland City Council.

"Our Ashland City Council is no different from most city councils in Wisconsin," says Mary. "We are often split right down the middle when we vote, and I thought it was a long shot to get all 11 members of our council to pass a resolution with the word 'eco' in it, let alone pass it unanimously. So I set up a special showing of my slideshow in the City Council chambers before the vote took place." One of the conservative council members spoke after Mary's presentation about his love of fishing in Lake Superior. Mary continues, "He is an avid hunter and fisherman. He said that he had recently been tested for mercury poisoning, and he found out that he had the 31st highest level of mercury toxicity in the state! He was angry that mercury advisories weren't posted at the boat landing. After his story, it felt natural that the vote was unanimous."

More local governments are getting on board. The City Council of Bayfield and the Town Board of Bayfield have also passed eco-

TOWARD A HEALTHY PLANET

municipality resolutions that commit their local entities to following ecological guidelines in purchasing and energy-use decisions. The Bad River Band of the Lake Superior Tribe of Chippewa Indians has adopted a Tribal Energy Plan to enable the community to move toward energy independence. The Alliance for Sustainability, a 14-year-old local nonprofit, has raised enough public and private support to open a "Sustainable Chequamegon Center" and hire a full-time coordinator to keep track of all the good ideas in the region and put people in touch with each other. Study circles in peoples' homes to discuss books on sustainability and figure out creative ideas for working together are commonplace throughout the bay area.

Swedish eco-municipality leaders made two visits to the Chequamegon Bay in the winter and summer of 2005. Both events drew participants from many communities in and around the Bay— Bad River (Odanah), Ashland, Washburn, Bayfield, Red Cliff and LaPointe. "Their summer presentation in the Big Top Chautauqua tent was a particularly magical evening," Mary says. "The Swedes not only received a standing ovation that night, but it took place on the summer solstice (Midsummer's Eve in Scandinavia), and we had heard they might be homesick for their midnight bonfires and celebrations. So we took them to a gathering afterwards—and there we were under a full moon with fireflies all around, sharing music until all hours of the morning. Once again, we all seemed to be in the right place at the right time." In the summer of 2006, a delegation of eight from the Bay visited Sweden to learn more.

Today the work of measuring how communities around the bay contribute to greenhouse gases is just beginning. Two community-wide outreach programs have really taken off. In a program aimed at citizens, college interns go door-to-door and talk with residents about how to save money and energy in their homes. They even offer compact fluorescent light bulbs to residents who are willing to take out their incandescent bulbs and screw in the energy saving bulbs.

For businesses, a "Green Team Network of Early Adopters of Sustainability" has formed to implement changes and share assessment techniques. The network already includes over a dozen businesses that range from the local food co-op to Walmart; from three city governments to BART, the local transportation company.

The area is burgeoning with initiatives. A "Travel Green" certification program launched by the state identified Bayfield as a pilot community. In the Washburn Elementary School, the principal is working with students and teachers to recycle, save paper, plant gardens and become a Department of Public Instruction certified "Green and Healthy School." Students in Ashland High School are making a DVD on energy-saving measures in their school. Bretting Manufacturing, H Windows and Northland College have won recognition for their ecological practices. A network of food producers and consumers has set up a Mobile Farmers' Market, Native American gardening projects and buying clubs for meat.

There have been all sorts of local theories as to why this movement has taken hold in the Chequamegon Bay area. Some think it's because the small communities around the Bay can see each others' lights at night. Some believe that the love for a pristine region that is the gateway to the Apostle Islands National Lakeshore and the Chequamegon-Nicolet National Forest provides the foundation for the enthusiasm.

Mary summarizes her thoughts on the area's success. "It's all about making our good ideas visible to each other. Several of us speak regularly to other rural communities about the importance of collaborating in a rural area. One small town doesn't have the resources to do a whole lot. What many people don't fully understand yet is that we are part of a global movement of local environmental initiatives. We are changing the world one region at a time and sharing our successes as we go along."

POWERING THE WAY
LAKE MICHIGAN WIND AND SUN, STURGEON BAY

Spinning with the steady winds that sweep over the shores of Lake Michigan in Door County are the blades of several wind turbines. They are the pillars of an energy future that does not rely on fossil fuels and does not pollute the water or air. Located in an old farmhouse outside of Sturgeon Bay, Lake Michigan Wind and Sun bustles with activity. John and Ann Hippensteel, who own the 25-year-old company, stay busy responding to the rapidly growing interest in renewable energy systems, both throughout the state and around the world.

Located on a 40-acre farmstead, which was once a small-scale dairy operation, the company offers system design, engineering and consulting services for renewable energy projects. It also operates as a dealer for some of the leading small- and large-scale renewable energy systems. Since 1981, the company has been providing small wind turbine and renewable energy systems and selling a variety of components for these systems such as solar thermal panels, solar electric modules, batteries and inverters.

Solar electric and solar thermal systems help power and heat what is now a fabrication shop and mechanical and electronics repair facility. Another component of the business supplies custom blades and replacement parts for home-sized wind electric systems manufactured as early as the 1930s.

"I've been interested in environmentally sound power production since my days as a student at the University of Copenhagen, where I participated in anti-nuclear demonstrations," shares John. "Denmark is a country that has a ban on nuclear plants and new coal plants." After getting a degree in mechanical engineering and working with the Peace Corps in "appropriate technology," John transplanted these experiences and this perspective back home to Wisconsin.

"We have an ideal site for wind and solar, high on the bluff within sight of Lake Michigan." John and Ann moved the business 20 miles east from former owner Mick Sagrillo's farm, to their present location. Explains John, "This location is also fairly close to my wife's family, and although renewable energy is very important, family is more important." Structured as a C-corporation, Lake Michigan Wind and Sun relies on two full-time and six part-time employees, as well as several highly experienced subcontracted service technicians who seem to almost enjoy climbing 120-foot towers to do routine maintenance and service checks on existing operational systems.

"It has not always been easy to make a living doing what we believe in," admits John. "Renewable energy systems are still quite expensive. When we talk to people we always counsel them to invest in energy efficiency and conservation before spending any money on renewable energy equipment." The present increase in business is due to people's heightened awareness of the importance of producing clean energy, aided by dramatic increases in fuel prices. Combining this with recent state and federal incentives helps people

to move ahead with projects they believe in and can now better afford. "It would be nice to take a day off now and then, but a business is like having kids, it's a 24/7 operation," smiles John, who has a tough time being negative about a livelihood he loves with a passion. His four kids, ranging in age from 11 to 21 years, can't help but be involved with the business, similar to the family that farmed at the present homestead from the 1800s to about 1980.

As all savvy businesspersons do to ensure long-term viability, John and Ann have diversified their company to cover many facets of the renewable energy industry: providing site assessments, system design, part re-manufacturing, engineering consulting and servicing of operating systems. "We are a registered engineering firm in the state of Wisconsin that also does construction," he adds. "This provides us with well-rounded experience. Because of our expertise in solar electric, solar thermal and wind energy, we have no trouble keeping very busy."

"Our measure of success is severalfold, with our primary measure being able to provide an impact on the energy production in our society, while having satisfied customers," shares John. "Our success is also measured by whether or not we can sustain our family of six and still make the next mortgage payment. And we are successful." A large part of the success of the company is the reality that the renewable energy equipment now on the market is both more reliable and cost effective for businesses and homeowners to install. More than 50 percent of his business comes from small businesses based in rural areas, businesses with the space and resources to add a wind turbine and/or solar system to reduce energy costs.

Examples of businesses adopting renewable energy systems abound, like the 10 kilowatt wind turbine and 12 kilowatt solar electric systems installed by Lake Michigan Wind and Sun for TDL Electronics in rural Racine County. Owner Tom Leitshuh invested in this technology to power his business, which is located in a restored two-story dairy barn. TDL Electronics produces enough power to run the business, power the electric tractors and sell the excess to the utility. "Down the road from Tom is New Vision Farm, an organic hog farm that also recycles telephone poles into quality lumber," adds John. "This farm is owned by John and Laurel Shea who have plans to add a 12 kilowatt solar electric system to offset their energy costs. John and Laurel have owned a wind turbine for over ten years and were the inspiration for Tom Leitshuh's project."

"In addition to designing and installing renewable energy systems, we also live and work in the middle of our own test laboratory, producing two to three times more electricity than we use," says John, knowing that this aspect of the business makes it possible for them to provide better service and products to their customers, while also helping the whole industry. If you stop by his workshop, he'll run the output numbers and show you the results. The demonstration and testing of renewable energy equipment presently includes a 20 kilowatt Jacobs 31/20, a 1 kilowatt Southwest Energy H-80, a 2.5 kilowatt Proven and a 1.5 kilowatt African Wind Power—and these are just some of his wind turbines. There are also three solar electric, or photovoltaic, systems with modules made by Shell, BP and United Solar, totaling 3 kilowatts in rated output, along with a solar hot water heating system and an in-floor radiant solar thermal system that heats the shop. "We certainly provide more energy than we need and rather than sell the excess, we donate the surplus to help offset the bills of people less fortunate or those with financial difficulties," he adds.

When he's not out on projects in the Midwest or halfway around the world, John devotes resources and energy to his neighborhood. "On the small scale, we've taken over a non-working farm and turned it into a wind and solar farm, generating over 30,000 kilowatt hours annually," explains John. "It helps when the public utility pays $0.225 per kilowatt hour for your solar energy, as is the case with Wisconsin Energy's solar buyback program. On occasion,

we also help the neighbors with equipment repair for agricultural equipment. Our fabrication and machine shop equipment is ideally suited for this."

Education and experience is key to the success of Lake Michigan Wind and Sun. "An engineering degree, along with a liberal arts education and construction and industry experience to get me through school has brought us to where we are today," says John. "We can't rule out the importance of just plain desire to accomplish our goals, since this driving force makes us learn what we need to succeed." Lake Michigan Wind and Sun has worked with many educational groups such as the Midwest Renewable Energy Association (MREA) and environmental groups around the country and abroad. "We teach classes every year at the MREA's Renewable Energy and Sustainable Living Fair," continues John. "Last year we taught classes in Mexico and the year before in Northern Ireland. This work abroad helps to provide a wonderful education for our children, providing insight to other cultures and helping to make the world smaller."

As for the future of the renewable energy industry, Lake Michigan Wind and Sun hopes to encourage greater local entrepreneurship related to contractors working with property owners to service, maintain or expand their systems. "As the market develops," explains John, "we see potential in assisting other contractors in the industry so that expertise can be more local." In the spirit of having decentralized, democratic, locally owned power producers (e.g., indiviudals or small businesses) using wind and solar as their energy sources, the very industry can mimic this pattern and support local economic growth.

One thing is certain, with rising energy costs and enhanced concern for the environment, Lake Michigan Wind and Sun has the experience, know-how and power to ride the winds of change. Energy independence can be only a solar panel or turbine away and John and Ann's company can guide the way.

TRAVEL & RECREATION

Wisconsin's countryside is rich in natural beauty, art, culture and history, which make it an alluring place for tourists and locals alike. An abundance of surprises await the traveler willing to venture beyond the bustling cities and off the main paths. Wisconsin's rural gems offer unique, authentic experiences and unparalleled hospitality.

At the enchanting lodgings showcased in this chapter, your hosts not only provide comfortable accommodations, but also educate and inspire you through their green building design, alternative energy use and incorporation of fresh, locally grown foods into their menus. Each is situated in a beautiful setting—from the shore of Lake Superior, to a hobby farm, to 200 acres of a once-active dairy farm.

We also share the stories of two remarkable trails. The first, a hiking trail, follows the path of an elusive glacier and represents a remarkable collaboration among landowners and government entities. The second trail provides a road map to the plentiful shops, historic sites, artists studios and small farms that are tucked away throughout the northwestern counties. Here travelers can behold or purchase the handmade and homegrown, from pottery to paintings, from preserves to honey wine.

A GLACIAL EXPERIENCE
THE ICE AGE TRAIL, CROSSING WISCONSIN

Around 10,000 years ago the mile-high wall of ice, known as the Wisconsin Glacier and responsible for shaping much of Wisconsin's physical landscape, began to melt. In its wake, the retreating ice deposited a line of sediment along its southern edge, a serpentine strip of gravelly hills called a terminal moraine that defined the glacier's final reach across the state. Extending like a ribbon from St. Croix Falls in Polk County to Potawatomi State Park in Door County, this scenic belt preserves the memory of Wisconsin's geologic past. Since 1958, thousands of Wisconsin residents have been working to protect, preserve and share this past through the creation of a continuous 1,200-mile-long footpath along the glacier's edge.

The Ice Age National Scenic Trail, commissioned by Congress in 1980, snakes through forests, farms, prairies and communities— large and small—in 30 Wisconsin counties. Carved from land both privately and publicly owned, the trail is currently more than half-finished, with about 600 of the proposed 1,200 miles completed. It is one of only two National Scenic Trails that is contained within one state.

"The diversity of environments across the trail is incredible and unlike any other park in existence," says Mike Wollmer, president of the Ice Age Park and Trail Foundation. "From the heavily glaciated Kettle Moraine in the southeast to the forests of Taylor County and the lakeshore beach by Lake Michigan, the trail runs through all of it."

The idea for a trail began with Milwaukee attorney Raymond Zillmer, an avid outdoorsman and leading advocate for the protection of the Kettle Moraine State Forest in the 1930s and 1940s. Zillmer envisioned the Kettle Moraine as the nucleus of a much larger linear park that would follow the path of the continent's most recent glaciation. Recognizing that the glacier had shaped not only the state's physical landscape, but also its cultural landscape, he believed that a trail would help connect residents to nature as well as their geologic past. In 1958, Zillmer founded the Ice Age Park and Trail Foundation to begin efforts to establish the trail as a national park.

Ray Zillmer's dream was long in coming, however. The National Park Service, while acknowledging the significance of the terrain, concluded that a park hundreds of miles long would be too difficult to administer. Undeterred, trail advocates came up with an alternative, the Ice Age National Scientific Reserve, an affiliated area of the National Park System. Comprised of nine separate units, President Lyndon Johnson signed the reserve into law in 1964. Throughout the 1970s, volunteers constructed new trail segments, incorporated older trails into the system, and worked to secure additional parcels of land. Finally, in 1980, the Ice Age Trail joined the National Trails System, a system that includes the Appalachian and the Pacific Crest trails, and Ray Zillmer's vision seemed at last fulfilled.

Today, the Ice Age Trail is administered by the National Park Service, the Wisconsin Department of Natural Resources (DNR) and the Ice Age Park and Trail Foundation. But unlike the Appalachian Trail, where the National Park Service has taken the lead in acquiring land, the Park Service does not have the authority to purchase the nationally significant glacial features that the trail is intended to preserve. Instead, the Wisconsin DNR and the Foundation purchase land using donated funds and government grants from sources like the Knowles-Nelson Stewardship Program and the Dane County Conservation Fund.

The heart of the Ice Age Trail, however, lies in the generosity of private landowners without whom the trail would not exist— landowners like Dean Dversdall. Ten years ago, a friend approached Dean about putting the trail through a portion of his 92 acres in Polk County. He agreed, and today Dean is one of the

roughly 30 private landowners in the county who have made a "handshake agreement" with the Foundation to allow public access to the trail. Dean also serves as coordinator of the Indianhead Chapter of the Ice Age Park and Trail Foundation, which oversees a region of some 60 miles at the western terminus of the trail in Polk County.

"The trail makes it so easy for anyone to get out into nature and enjoy the beauty of the region," Dean says. "Being a part of the trail was an easy decision."

What makes the Ice Age Trail unique is the involvement of the communities along its route. Unlike other trails, the Ice Age Trail is designed to connect towns, not avoid them. In fact, 57 percent of Wisconsin's residents live within 20 miles of the trail.

St. Croix Falls is one of many towns that have enthusiastically embraced the Ice Age Trail. So much so that the town is now known as "The City of Trails," named for the ten trails located within city limits. Ed Emerson, city administrator for the town, says the Ice Age Trail opened the town's eyes to the natural assets all around them. "St. Croix Falls is inextricably tied to the outdoors. We have the river and the craggy bluffs that dramatically showcase the effects of the ice age," Ed says. "And environmentalist Gaylord Nelson is our town son."

Once the town embraced the trail, the natural links to the river and to Nelson's environmental legacy became obvious, says Ed. St. Croix Falls has since been exploring ways to become a more sustainable community, incorporating, for example, more green building features onto city property and partnering with the Ice Age Park and Trail Foundation and the Nature Conservancy, among others, to preserve natural areas. In 2005, St. Croix Falls dedicated a 76-acre regional park to Raymond Zillmer in honor of his vision for the trail.

The town has also seen an uptick in tourism. Sue Matthews, director of the Polk County Information Center, receives more calls and inquiries about the trail each year. "We're really proud to say that the western terminus of the Ice Age Trail is here in St. Croix Falls," she says. "And more and more people, realizing all that we have to offer, are coming to experience our trails as well as our flourishing arts community as a result."

Community involvement, along with the dedication of thousands of volunteers each year, has been vital to the continued growth and support of the Ice Age Trail since it began. But challenges remain and the trail continues to be a work in progress.

Many of the handshake agreements with private landowners are lost with changing land uses. Urbanization has also made the acquisition of new land parcels difficult. Land prices continue to rise, making funding a persistent struggle for the Foundation. In 1987, the state of Wisconsin designated the trail as Wisconsin's only State Scenic Trail to help curb some of the rerouting and reconstruction problems that have plagued its development. The state has since permanently protected 7,000 acres of land for the trail. The Ice Age Park and Trails Foundation has itself acquired more than 3,000 acres of land over the decades.

Despite the Ice Age Trail's fragmented existence, the land that it crosses contains a vast and important history that the people and communities along its path are determined to preserve. "This trail means so much to so many people of all ages and backgrounds," says Mike. "It's a unique opportunity for people in Wisconsin and throughout the region to understand the ways the land has shaped our human experience and to engage in the natural world all around us."

HARVESTING THE GOOD LIFE

INN SERENDIPITY BED & BREAKFAST AND FARM, BROWNTOWN

To co-owners John Ivanko and Lisa Kivirist, their 5.5-acre hobby farm, ecotourism and agritourism enterprises and creative services marketing company all share something in common. The goal of their diversified operations is not about earning money but, rather, about creating a more fulfilling life. They believe their interconnected businesses have a triple bottom line: profits, yes, but also meeting ecological and social priorities.

Located outside Monroe, the award-winning Inn Serendipity Bed & Breakfast—recognized as one of the "top ten eco-destinations in North America" by *Natural Home* magazine—is powered by 100 percent renewable energy and is Travel Green Wisconsin certified. Its innkeepers serve vegetarian breakfasts to their guests, prepared mostly with ingredients from the farm's organic gardens.

Lisa and John are not renewable energy experts, nor did they grow up as farmers. Hailing from suburban upbringings—Lisa from Chicago and John from Detroit—this husband-and-wife team settled on the farm in 1996 because of the opportunities it held to craft a

livelihood that was truer to their values and interests. They're representative of what some researchers have called "lifestyle migrants," emphasizing quality of life over size of bank account.

"We realized that while we said we valued family, friends and wholesome food, we lived and worked in ways that denied us what we yearned for," says Lisa, her young son, Liam, close by. "Raising our son, being outside in the gardens, eating fresh, local food and having time to spend with friends and family were more important than the bi-monthly paycheck. Moving to the farm gave us a chance to do the things we enjoyed while caring for the planet and our community."

Besides operating the bed and breakfast, the couple rent out a cabin in the woods in Vernon County, write books, consult on marketing topics, speak at a wide range of venues about conservation and sustainable living and occasionally sell surplus vegetables, fruits and herbs at a farmers' market in Madison. John is a free-lance photographer for numerous magazines including *Mother Earth News*, *Hobby Farms* and *Wisconsin Trails*. Out of the upstairs bedroom that serves as

TRAVEL & RECREATION

their home office, the duo manage a diversity of endeavors that vary by the season—in much the same way as the foods they now eat from their garden.

"Our goal with our operations is to be fossil-fuel free and significantly more self-reliant than we were when we worked for a large advertising agency that offered one paycheck, one job title and lots of stress," smiles John. "By downsizing our operations and making them human-scaled, locally-based and more ecologically sound, we discovered economic self-reliance." To meet even more of their food needs (presently they grow about 70 percent), they're working on growing year-round in their active-solar-heated greenhouse, insulated with straw bales. With an entrepreneurial spirit, John's previous endeavors ranged from restaurant start-ups to marketing consulting. As his photography and writing developed, he started co-authoring award-winning children's photobooks with Maya Ajmera, executive director of the Global Fund for Children, that include: *To Be a Kid*, *To Be an Artist*, *Animal Friends* and *Be My Neighbor*.

"At any given time, we have at least five or six business activities going on," adds Lisa, who matured as an entrepreneur in her 20s, with work for Earth Day Chicago and event marketing for various clients. "One day we're sharing a campfire with bed and breakfast guests, the next day we're completing an article on deadline, weeding the gardens, teaching a cooperative pre-school class with other families in the community and finishing up the day with follow-up phone calls to the media for the Monroe Chamber of Commerce and

Industry. Our life is quite diversified, both in projects and income." Set up under an umbrella S-corporation, JDI Enterprises, Inc., the many complementary enterprises cultivated by Lisa and John keep them learning, growing and connected to the land, their community and the planet. Their hospitality businesses—the bed and breakfast and cabin rental—account for about 50 percent of their annual income as a business and provide the funds to turn back around to help pay for the conservation and restoration activities on the land. At the 30-acre cabin property, a riparian buffer of mostly hardwood trees was planted next to a stream that passes through their land.

Akin to the way businesses were commonly operated before the corporate culture became widespread, Inn Serendipity and Lisa and John's other enterprises are integrated with the family's lifestyle. While receipts and documentation are extensively kept for the IRS and tax purposes, many of the household's daily activities seem to blend from one thing to another. "We've developed our own sense of a work style," explains Lisa.

"So much of what we are able to do today is a result of the ever more powerful computers and the rapid expansion of the Internet," admits John. "Also, there was a time when we worked out of our downtown apartment in Chicago and had to hide the fact that we were self-employed. Now—with the chickens clucking in the background—calling a magazine editor in New York City offers a more acceptable and memorable connection. Businesses and the nonprofit community have increasingly embraced subcontracting projects out to freelancers and free agents, in much the same way that outsourcing has caught on. It saves them money but offers us lots of control over our schedule and projects."

"Our strategy has been to develop a farm-based livelihood that balances our consideration of food systems, energy systems, living systems and livelihood in a way that can sustain us and help heal the land, clean the air and purify the water," continues Lisa. "From our wind turbine to the straw bale greenhouse, from the organic gardening strategies to co-parenting our son, we're constantly evolving our endeavors as we seek to recreate the good life in the twenty-first century. We've also rediscovered our interdependency with our community, both local and regional. Mentors, neighbors and expertise from nonprofit organizations like the Midwest Renewable Energy Association have made our journey possible."

Documented at length in their book, *Rural Renaissance: Renewing the Quest for the Good Life*, Lisa and John have woven together these four main aspects that define their ever-evolving journey. Their cookbook, *Edible Earth*, offers recipes that showcase the simple,

creative and budget-friendly side to eating lower on the food chain. In terms of renewable energy, they've added a 10 kilowatt Bergey wind turbine, a 0.7 kilowatt photovoltaic system, woodstove for heat, two solar thermal systems—for domestic hot water and to heat their greenhouse—and they're making their own biodiesel in partnership with their neighbors for back-up heating systems. They even have a 1974 electric CitiCar that's plugged into a photovoltaic power station on site and used for short-distance commuting. Due to their comprehensive use of renewable energy systems and sustainable living strategies, Inn Serendipity is an Energy Star Small Business, a Co-op America Business Network member, certified as a Travel Green Wisconsin accommodation and is on the National Solar Tours.

"We've joined thousands of others in reframing what it means to be farmers and entrepreneurs in America," says John. "Instead of commodity crops, we're harvesting wind and solar energy, growing our food with no synthetic chemicals and re-creating commerce in a way that sustains us and the planet."

Four Seasons of Fun
Justin Trails Resort, Sparta

At Justin Trails Resort, owners Donna and Don Justin dish up more than hearty fare at their bed and breakfast. Located on over 200 acres in Sparta, Justin Trails Resort provides a buffet of rural recreational opportunities blended with luxury amenities that keep their guests engaged and returning for more. The Justins' openness to new ideas and change enabled these dairy farmers to reinvent their farm as a tourist attraction and recreation-based resort. Evidence of success includes national honors for the "Most Romantic Inn" by *Travel America* and "Best place to take the family" by *Family Life*.

"In the mid 1980s, we started seeing the writing on the wall for the agriculture industry and knew we needed to start doing something other than farming if we were to keep our land," explains Donna. Attending the 1986 Farm and Ranch Congress in St. Louis solidified this feeling. "After hearing all the sad stories of farm foreclosures and the small farmer going down the tubes, we came home motivated to start diversifying in order to keep this land that has been in Don's family since 1916."

The Justins' first agritourism venture, which opened in 1985, created cross-country ski trails through the farm's 150 wooded acres. Donna and Don realized that people who came to use the trails would need a place to stay, so they opened four bedrooms in their farmhouse in 1986 as a bed and breakfast, making Justin Trails one of the first licensed bed and breakfasts in Wisconsin.

From then on a detailed, well-researched, business plan proved to be the heart of Justin Trails Resort's success. New to running a tourism business, Donna tapped into state resources for assistance, enrolling in a program through the Wisconsin Development Authority to write the business plan in 1990. As part of their research, Donna and Don visited other bed and breakfasts for ideas and perspectives. They also tapped into trend data and resources from national organizations such as the Professional Association of Innkeepers International. "We researched and wrote a specific plan, growing the business slowly and adding new elements every couple of years," explains Donna. "The plan helped us take into account and be prepared for bigger maintenance and upkeep projects, such as putting in a larger septic system."

Sensing national tourism trends of increases in both family travelers as well as romantic bed and breakfast goers, both of which could be attracted by stand-alone units outside the main farmhouse, the Justins added three cabins to their property. Their first cabin project in 1990 involved the renovation of an old granary outbuilding into cottage lodging. This was followed by building two stand-alone log cabins—first "Little House" and then "Paul Bunyan." In 1996, a machine shed that had been a bunkhouse and lodge space was upgraded into a commercial kitchen, providing space and facilities to cater to family reunions, retreats, special events and day-trippers on bus tours as well as bed and breakfast guests' breakfasts.

Donna takes pride in creating breakfasts that showcase local foods. "Our eggs come from a neighboring farm and we organically grow the potatoes and onions in our garden. When we explain to our guests that we serve cranberry juice as cranberries are grown in our area, folks gain a new understanding and appreciation of these things," explains Donna.

The Justin's strategic focus on their business plan led them to transition out of farming and other off-farm jobs. They sold the dairy herd to a local Amish farm in 1996 and sold the remaining farm equipment in 1998. While focused on their tourism business, Donna and Don haven't lost their farm connection and agritourism experience. An array of animals can be found in the barns and fields, including llamas, goats and two Siberian Huskies. The Huskies provide winter guests a unique dogsled experience. "We're still working our land and running the family farm business, just in a different way than raising crops or livestock," Don adds.

The seasonality emphasis of Justin Trails Resort provides reasons for guests to return throughout the year. Eight miles of cross-country winter ski trails, as well as snowshoeing trails and hills for snow tubing, turn into prime hiking spots during the summer. Don maintains the trails with a Scandik snowmobile. Beautifully landscaped gardens, as well as open areas for softball or volleyball, inspire guests to linger on the grounds and reconnect with family and friends.

A two-story playhouse "arrived" at Justin Trails Resort. "The kids of some long-time guests of ours, from the Chicago suburbs, had outgrown the playhouse and they didn't know what to do with it," explains Donna. "We bartered bed and breakfast lodging with them for the playhouse and Don rebuilt it on the farm. Now this family's grandchildren can come and have a connection to Justin Trails," Donna adds with a smile.

Such ongoing relationships with families returning for annual visits have created a reliable customer base. "We have two families that have had a standing reservation here the first weekend in February for over a dozen years. This weekend is the only time during the year they all get together. It's rewarding for me to watch the kids grow up with a strong connection to our farm."

What keeps Donna and Don fresh and energized after nearly two decades in the tourism business? "We always try to have something new going on, keeping ahead of national tourism trends," Don comments. Attending national bed and breakfast and cross-country ski owners' conferences connects them with emerging trends. "Tourism trends tend to start on the west and east coasts and then migrate to the Midwest. By hearing what people in California or New York are doing, we can stay ahead of the curve," adds Donna. Larger bed and breakfast rooms with whirlpools and fireplaces were concepts from the coasts that Donna and Don incorporated at Justin Trails, creating suites out of the existing rooms. It differentiates their rooms from other Midwestern bed and breakfasts.

Keeping active in leadership roles in various organizations also keeps the Justins engaged with new ideas. Donna served as the first state president of the Wisconsin Bed & Breakfast Association, now one of the largest state bed and breakfast groups in the country, as well as in various leadership positions with the National Association of Women Business Owners and the Wisconsin Agricultural Tourism Association.

Even with a thought-out business plan and strategic vision, Donna and Don remain open to and relish the serendipitous side of running a business. Take disc golf, for example. A student intern from an area university came to Justin Trails to research different recreational opportunities. "I was flipping through some of her books and came across a description of disc golf, which is similar in concept to golf but played with Frisbees and baskets," explains Don. "I thought to myself, we can do this. We didn't need to invest a lot to start a course, nor did we need a lot of land. A nine-basket course runs on five acres. Kind of one of those, 'Build it and they will come' ideas," Don adds, with his characteristically warm chuckle. Today Justin Trails Resort has two 18-basket disc golf courses and has become a destination for disc golf fans, hosting regular disc golf tournaments.

Both national and local media have embraced Justin Trails Resort's story, from area newspapers to a *USA Today* feature on family-friendly destinations. A three-inch thick binder of clippings contains all the media coverage from over the years. "We've realized the importance of always keeping our story fresh and new to garner media interest," explains Donna.

The Justins have also learned to listen to feedback from writers and journalists, which resulted in their current name, Justin Trails Resort. "We originally named the place 'Just-N-Trails,' playing off the name of our boat, 'Just-N-Fun,'" explains Donna. "But 'N-Trails' sounded just like 'entrails,' and that was not a good image. One journalist even asked us what 'just guts' means. So, when we officially incorporated in 1998, we simplified our name to Justin Trails."

Don summarizes the Justin Trails Resort story with a wink and a smile: "Guess we learned that people would pay more to come visit our land than we'd get farming it."

HANDMADE AND HOMEGROWN
WISCONSIN'S NORTHWEST HERITAGE PASSAGE

A blank space on the map means adventure to those who like to explore, but when Alene Peterson sees the blank space that is northwest Wisconsin on most guidebook maps, she just gets mad.

"Nobody knows we're here," she explains of her home region. "We were just marketing the water, fishing and hunting." Up until their recent retirement, Alene and her husband, Norm, owned and operated Northwinds Book and Fiber in Spooner, a bookstore with a regional focus that also serves as a market and meeting place for local artists and craftspeople. She is well-acquainted with guidebooks and travelogues on Wisconsin. Pulling a typical sample off the shelf, she opens it to the inevitable map in the front. "Look," she says, pointing to a Wisconsin state map that lists points of interest everywhere except in the northwest. "I was tired of getting books in that looked like that. Time after time after time."

But that's changing since Alene and a small group of determined volunteers founded the Wisconsin's Northwest Heritage Passage (WNHP) in 2000. The full-color "Handmade and Homegrown" brochure, printed and distributed by the nonprofit organization, describes more than 150 artists, craftspeople, historic sites and farms offering homegrown products in 13 northwest Wisconsin

counties, along with a map to guide visitors through this cornucopia of regional treasures.

"We've printed about 77,000 (brochures) so far," says WNHP president Jerry Boucher, a professional photographer and designer who owns and operates School House Productions in Clear Lake. "And we've got about 5,000 left. The awareness of it is really high. We got a letter after the first map came out from the lady who manages the gift shop at the Red Cliff Indian Reservation. She said that had been their best year yet, and many people came with the map in hand."

Others have taken notice, too. The WNHP has been named one of the top ten Rural Initiatives in Wisconsin by the state's Department of Tourism, and received the 2004 "Trailblazer Award" from the Wisconsin Association of Convention and Visitors Bureaus. Media coverage has included feature articles in *Wisconsin West* magazine and in the statewide rural newspaper, *The Country Today*.

The group is not resting on its laurels. Current plans are to print an updated brochure in 2007 and publish a comprehensive guidebook in 2009. Explains Jerry, "We all face the same thing. If you have an event or product, there's not any way to let people know about it.

WNHP is aimed at getting people who are looking for those products to people who are producing these things. Within an hour of our route we've got four million people in the Minneapolis/St. Paul area, and even within our region a lot of people don't know the artists next door to them. If the map and book can change that so there's a higher level of awareness, it's got to help everybody."

Making these plans a reality will depend on finding more volunteers willing to discover, visit, photograph, write and compile listings for the area's artisans. It will also depend on finding additional funding. Costs for printing the brochure have so far been covered by $1,000 contributions from each of the participating counties, a Joint Effort

Marketing grant from the state Department of Tourism, and contributions from Excel Energy and private individuals. Even more critical than finding future funding is finding more volunteers, Jerry notes. "Identifying all these artists is a tremendous task, and the success of the project is going to depend a lot on volunteers."

Though the future of the project is not yet crystal clear, the groundwork has been well laid, based on the success of a similar group in the Appalachian Mountains. Alene says she got the idea for the WNHP while driving the Blue Ridge Parkway in the Appalachians in 1999. "It's a very craft-rich area," she explains, but the local artists and craftspeople live away from the main

traffic corridors, just as in northwest Wisconsin. That problem was solved by an organization called HandMade in America, which publishes *The Craft Heritage Trails of Western North Carolina* guidebook to the region's artisans.

"I came home with that book and said, 'You guys—look what I found!' That's how this got started," Alene comments. "We really were becoming aware of how many people were off in the woods doing wonderful things in terms of art. What we're trying to do with this is identify, in these 13 northwest counties, the art, the crafts, the heritage and the niche agriculture. These things appeal to the same people. We started with Highway 63 because it still goes through the small towns. That route gives an opportunity to stop and see things along the way."

The WNHP name was carefully chosen, Alene says. "We chose to call it the 'Passage' because it's not just a road trip, it's an experience. 'Heritage' is the agriculture and crafts—it's part of what we are. And 'Northwest' because that's where we are."

To have a listing in the WNHP brochure, a studio, farm or workshop must meet certain criteria, Alene explains. "It needs to be a quality product. And the idea of the map and book is to send people to people's houses, so we have to think of safety and accessibility." That means the driveway, steps and public areas

must meet standards. Lastly, not all artisans keep regular hours for the visiting public, Alene adds, "and we have struggled with that. Do we put on places that are only open by appointment?"

Due to the number of sites and the limited brochure space, artists and farms that don't keep regular hours will probably be dropped from the updated brochure, Alene says. But the book will include them. "There are some artists in the area whose work is known on a national basis, but may not have anything for sale in this area and aren't looking for people to come down their driveway," she notes. But, she adds, even those artists benefit from a listing, through raised awareness among potential customers within the region.

At its heart, that's what WNHP is about: improving the customer base for the area's artists, craftspeople and small farmers. "A lot of artists and niche ag people want to move to an area that they like, and if this project helps support them and allows them to work where they want to be, and make a living at it, then I think it's a very important project," Jerry concludes.

Alene adds, "I've often felt, since 1999, that I've had a tiger by the tail. But you meet the people, you know what they have to offer, and you wish more people knew about them. It's a great deal of fun."

DOING WELL BY DOING GOOD
Pinehurst Inn at Pikes Creek Bed & Breakfast, Bayfield

Near the shores of Lake Superior, nestled in the thriving northwoods community of Bayfield, Pinehurst Inn at Pikes Creek Bed & Breakfast reflects the natural beauty and thrives in the vibrant local community of which it plays a contributing part. With eight luxury guest rooms split between the eco-renovated 1885 Main Historic House and the newly constructed green-design and naturally built Garden House, owners Nancy and Steve Sandstrom don't exaggerate when they exclaim it's easy to be green.

While operated as a bed and breakfast since 1984, Pinehurst Inn sprouted up as a new model for more sustainable design and business operation after Nancy and Steve purchased the inn in 1995. The pillars and sandstone of the Main House and pristine shoreline and abundant lighthouses in the Bayfield area were very familiar to Nancy, who grew up spending every summer in Bayfield, often staying with her distant cousins who owned the house. So settling down in the thriving college and tourism-based area was as natural as the freshly baked hot biscuits covered in locally tapped maple syrup that Nancy remembered savoring every summer during her childhood visits.

Nancy and Steve join millions of other rural lifestyle migrants, seeking solace in the fresh air, inviting small town community life and opportunity to live in ways more reflective of their passions. "We were both ready for a lifestyle change," explains Steve. "I was stressed out with working in a family printing business and Nancy was stressed out working in nonprofit management. We enjoyed staying at bed and breakfasts and we both thought it would be a more pleasant lifestyle."

So the couple, with kids now off on their own, set out to renovate the Main Historic House while adding a new guesthouse called the Garden House. At the forefront of every design consideration was reducing the ecological impacts. For example, the Garden House features interior trim made with local, sustainably harvested lumber, low-emissive thermopane energy-conserving windows, low-flow faucets and toilets that help conserve water, and fiber cement siding that is made with recycled material content. A solar thermal system captures the sun's warmth to heat the water in the Garden House and an innovative aerobic digester helps in treating sewage. Throughout the operations, energy-efficient Energy Star-certified appliances, biodegradable nontoxic cleaners, natural

and organic linens and recyclable and recycled products are used. Landscaping features native perennials and water catchment systems used for irrigation.

"We have taken a special historical property and helped make it more compatible with the Earth," explains Steve, who also works as the environmental outreach coordinator for the Sigurd Olson Environmental Institute at Northland College, a small liberal arts college in nearby Ashland, widely known for its environmental curriculum. "Our inn offers our guests examples of what they could do in their own homes to reduce their environmental footprint. We show them that you can make a difference without being radical."

In reality, being green was a lot of hard work. "We honestly felt that the spirit of this place carried us through the long process of creating our inn, making the renovations, the strenuous work and

the financial commitment," admits Nancy. "Frequently when feeling overwhelmed, I would find solace and a sense of peace among the huge white pines framing the house, or wander the shores of Lake Superior to hear the water's message of support."

It's not surprising that many of the nearly 2,000 guests who stay at the Pinehurst Inn each year share this same affinity for nature's embrace. Included with room accommodations is a delicious breakfast served in the Main House prepared with locally grown organic foods and produce, organic coffees and teas and "tender loving care." Many of the breakfasts showcase the regional fruits seasonally in abundance, most purchased directly from the farmers.

"Visitors really get into what we've done here," beams Nancy. "They are hungry for the information. Increasingly, they understand both the need for these steps and their value." The

Garden House Gathering Room is often filled with guests reviewing the renovation binders or reading literature or books offered for guests wishing to learn more about sustainable design, natural building, renewable energy or other related topics. Guests are even presented with a "Trees for Travel" certificate offered through the nonprofit organization Trees for the Future, helping guests offset transportation impacts through reforestation efforts facilitated by the organization.

"Our guests sense and appreciate our personal connection to the property, our historic connection as a family, our connection to the land, the big lake, gardens, surrounding woods and ravines," continues Nancy. "They share our appreciation of our sense of place and our efforts to preserve it through how we operate our business and volunteer in the community." Both Steve and Nancy are active with the Bayfield Regional Conservancy's Farmland Preservation Program and on a statewide basis in helping the Wisconsin Department of Tourism launch the Travel Green Wisconsin initiative, a statewide green travel certification program. Both are very involved in a regional eco-municipality movement as well.

When it comes to Pinehurst Inn's success, its definition is as diverse as the perennials found throughout the property. "We define success by a triple bottom line: people, place and profit," says Steve. "We look at not just the financial success, but also our personal health, the impact on employees, the education of our guests, the guest experience and our impact on the environment." The inn employs four part-time staff during the busy summer months, all local residents who share their vision.

Like a beacon found in one of the area's lighthouses, Pinehurst Inn has become both an early adopter of a more sustainable approach to running a business and an environmental advocate. "We have offered workshops to people interested in sustainable business, but the most important thing is that we lead by example," says Steve.

"The more we get recognized in the news, the more the people in the community learn about what we are doing. There is definitely a ripple effect."

Technology, whether the personal computer, the Internet or numerous new "green" building materials or renewable energy systems, like the solar thermal system that provides hot water for the guests' showers, makes creating a sustainable business in rural areas possible. "From the start, we've used a computer for record keeping, financial records and other business tasks," explains Nancy. "Our reservation system provides a well-rounded database of guests with information critical to good marketing. Our guest records contain more than address information. The records include their interests and activities they participated in while staying with us. Our website promotes the business while also providing additional information about our operations and business philosophy." The inn's web presence is extended through a monthly e-mail newsletter that maintains connections with guests while offering bits and pieces of education on sustainability.

"Our decision to locate the business here certainly relates to the familial connection to the property and the area," says Nancy. "We personally thrive on living in a small town and find being in a more rural location tends to feed both of our souls. This comes across to our guests. They get that we are totally connected to the property—whether the houses, gardens or community. This synergy is a critical part of what makes our business work. And it's what gives us joy."

Being green and doing well by doing good is a lot of hard work. "The days are incredibly long during our busy season and the work is physically taxing," explains Nancy. "What has surprised me is that I get intense joy at working hard. The work frequently doesn't feel like work." At Pinehurst Inn, it also comes in many shades of green.

GOOD ENOUGH TO EAT

Wisconsin is rich in entrepreneurs, many whose products are tied closely to the land. A place of innovators and risk takers, the fruits of these labors are successful businesses that generate pride among all. By producing award-winning products, these innovators bring the world's attention to the state's doorstep.

This chapter features a variety of businesses—from one of the country's leading organic companies to a small northern winery that makes delicious honey-based wine. Most are in the food business, producing amazing offerings like Berkshire pork chops, artisan cheeses and microbrewed beer. One business produces natural supplements and nutrition programs for livestock farmers.

Some of these businesses have grown beyond the borders of the state and others have chosen to keep a local or regional focus and serve a nearby community. The stories we share here highlight individuals, families and groups of people who have put their ideas on the table and taken risks to follow their dreams. Ingenuity, persistence, flexibility and vision are the background strengths each of these successful enterprises represents.

So next time you're looking for a great beer, wine, meat, cheese … —think Wisconsin.

Growing a National Movement
Organic Valley Family of Farms, La Farge

Nestled in the green hills of the Kickapoo Valley amidst a patchwork of lush coulees, growing fields and pasture, the Organic Valley Family of Farms' headquarters in La Farge blends into the bucolic scenery. And that's just how this cooperatively owned company wants it to be.

Despite being one of the nation's leading organic brands with over $333 million in sales in 2006, this organization's primary focus isn't about increasing profit and market share. Rather, their vision focuses on the health and well-being of farmer members, the land they steward and public education about the importance of sustainable agriculture and food choices. An inspirational success story worldwide, Organic Valley proves that businesses need not choose between profits and people—as they help revitalize family farms while revolutionizing the food business.

Back in 1988, a group of seven southwestern Wisconsin family farms joined forces to pool product, transportation, labor and other resources, forming a cooperative today called Cooperative Regions of Organic Producer Pools, or CROPP for short. "These founding Organic Valley farmers came together with a shared vision of working in partnership so that each of their families would stay on and derive income from their land," explains Jamie Johnson, Organic Valley's community relations manager.

Organic Valley's growth took off in the mid-1990s when the rBGH synthetic hormone was first introduced into conventional dairy production. "Consumers immediately wanted choices about what went into their milk and Organic Valley had an alternative to offer them," Jamie adds. "From then on, CROPP was on the map."

Still focused on a core base of dairy products, today Organic Valley boasts over 900 farmer-members from over 27 states and one Canadian province. This represents approximately 10 percent of the organic farming community in the United States. Producing over 200 different organic food products including milk, cheese, butter, eggs, soy, fruits, vegetables, juice and Organic Prairie brand meats, Organic Valley established a reputation early on as a trusted informational resource for their customers. In addition to Organic Valley's land ethic and business model, the bottom line of taste keeps customers loyal as well. For years, Organic Valley's cheese and butter products have consistently won top awards at the American Cheese

GOOD ENOUGH TO EAT

Society's annual judging competition, one of the world's most prestigious competitions for artisan and specialty cheesemaking.

Focusing on their website as a primary educational outreach tool, Organic Valley taps into experts ranging from pediatricians to chefs in order to keep consumers educated about organic. From healthy school lunch options for kids to "Mothers of Organic," an educational program helping parents make sound choices for their family, Organic Valley blends compelling graphics and photography with researched facts and tips to communicate lasting messages. Endearing profiles of Organic Valley farmers and slice-of-life photography pepper the website, putting a friendly, candid, real life face to the source of one's food.

Organic Valley's success remains deeply rooted in its cooperative business model. The difference between Organic Valley's cooperative structure and a traditional company lies in the way wealth is distributed. In a cooperative, all members share in the organization's success and decision-making process. When a farmer joins CROPP, the farmer establishes equity in the cooperative. He or she then has various opportunities to serve on governance and marketing committees, help determine pricing and receive numerous benefits—such as support for production, organic certification, farm planning, feed sourcing and veterinarian consulting. The growing organic market demand enables Organic Valley farmers to be paid 40 percent more than conventional farmers, resulting in increased opportunity for the long-term viability of family farms.

"The success of Organic Valley proves that organic agriculture can be a lifeline for America's struggling farms," says George Siemon, one of the founding Organic Valley farmers who now heads the cooperative. George refers to his position as that of the "C-E-I-E-I-O," a testament to the ongoing informal, fun-loving, hard-working nature of CROPP's employees and farmers. "In an era of rising and falling agricultural prices, Organic Valley employs a model that is unmatched anywhere on earth," he explains.

Organic Valley's Wisconsin roots remain a core component in the business today. Over 70 percent of the company's 300 employees live in the La Farge area, a strong economic boost to this village of 775 residents. The cooperative opened a new six million dollar, environmentally-friendly headquarters in 2004, utilizing creative green design approaches such as recycling cubicles from a dot-com business that went bust and stuffing the walls with insulation made from old, recycled blue jeans. Carpoolers and drivers of hybrid and biofuel vehicles garner the prime parking spots. CROPP's commitment to its rural roots will be further strengthened with the completion of a new state-of-the-art distribution center in nearby Cashton.

Perhaps not surprisingly, more Organic Valley farmers live in Wisconsin than any other state, an impact that brings Wisconsin to the forefront as a leader in the organic agriculture movement. Vernon County, where CROPP is based, holds the title of the county with the highest number of organic farmers in the nation. Organic Valley's Wisconsin base shines at their cooperative-sponsored Kickapoo Country Fair, an annual summer weekend that draws over 4,000 people for free educational workshops and entertainment on the grounds of the cooperative's headquarters. "We wanted to create a community event that brought people together to celebrate our shared rural heritage," Jamie explains. From tractor displays to local musicians to, of course, friendly cows, the July event resembles a family reunion as Organic Valley farmers mingle and their kids take to the dance floor.

Even with such a fun-loving, informal nature (you'll often find Organic Valley employees, and even CEIEIO George Siemon himself, in blue jeans and bare feet), hard work and visionary leadership remain the daily mantra for both employees and farmer members.

CROPP realizes and embraces the fact that there remains much work ahead to continue to drive the organic movement forward in a healthy manner. Current efforts focus on recruiting a new generation of farmers to the organic movement.

"America has lost about five million farmers since the 1930s and the average age of those who remain is 58 years old with only 6 percent of all farmers under the age of 35," Jamie explains. "These statistics helped prompt Organic Valley to create 'Generation Organic,' an educational outreach program encouraging and promoting the new generation of organic farmers, providing various resources such as educational workshops, mentoring and internship opportunities, and

financial and technical support for farmers transitioning to organic." These outreach and recruitment efforts assist Organic Valley's profits as well, since a steady stream of new CROPP farmers, 25 to 40 added annually, helps the cooperative keep up with the steadily increasing market demand for their products.

Organic Valley Family of Farms proves that two alternative business structures—the cooperative and the family farm—can blend together to grow into a profitable powerhouse within the food industry. With a dose of good, old-fashioned community building through education, Organic Valley is dedicated to supporting happy cows, happy farmers and happy customers.

Excellent, Earth-Friendly Cheeses
Cedar Grove Cheese, Plain

She looks familiar—vaguely. The pose is pure "Mona Lisa." But that face …

Staring placidly back from a package of award-winning cheese is the face of a sheep atop the figure of Mona Lisa. Somewhat surprising until you consider that Cedar Grove is the place where science and art meet—the cheesemaker's art, that is.

Cedar Grove Cheese, manufacturer of specialty and traditional cheeses, is located in the cascading hills of the driftless area just outside Plain. The company occupies a site that's been home to a cheese factory since 1878.

For many years, the factory produced mainly commodity cheese. But not too long after Bob Wills came on board as president in 1989, Cedar Grove faced a crisis. A customer who routinely bought most of Cedar Grove's product discontinued its purchases, and the company was left with more cheese than it could sell. Things looked bleak until another Wisconsin company, Swiss Colony, stepped in to purchase the surplus.

The episode marked a turning point in Cedar Grove's business philosophy, according to Bob, who holds a doctorate in economics. Building on a long-time interest in ecological and sustainable

farming, he decided to take the company in a new direction. Specialty markets, artisan cheeses and organics were areas that looked promising. And diversifying Cedar Grove's product line made good financial sense. No longer would the company be at the mercy of one large customer.

Today, more than a dozen years later, Cedar Grove has garnered a national reputation both for its excellent cheeses and its innovative, earth-friendly environmental practices. The industry publication *Cheese Market News* consistently cites it as one of the "50 Key Players" in the dairy industry.

The company is still small, employing a staff of 35, including six licensed cheesemakers—one of whom has been with the company since 1956. Every morning two Cedar Grove tank trucks pick up milk from 35 local farms, bringing in more than 140,000 pounds of milk, which by the next morning have been converted to around 14,000 pounds of cheese.

"This is one of the few businesses where there's a great mix of creativity and science. It's an exciting time to be an artisan cheesemaker," says Bob. Cedar Grove displayed a willingness to try new ideas early on by tapping into research showing consumers preferred the taste of dairy products from cows raised on grass

Open Aerobic
Tank 4

Open Aerobic
Tank 3

pastures. Cedar Grove helped develop a cheese from grass-fed cows that took "Best of Show" at the American Cheese Society in 2001, a year after the cheese was introduced.

Cheeses made from sheep's milk and combinations of sheep and cow's milk, such as "Mona," are newer projects underway with the Wisconsin Sheep Dairy Cooperative and University of Wisconsin–Madison researchers. In fact, "Dante," whose package features—you guessed it—a sheep's head perched on Rodin's "The Thinker," also took top honors in its class at the largest-ever

American Cheese Society competition in the summer of 2006. But even as it grows, keeping things local is at the heart of Cedar Grove's business. "I really like the local market," says Bob. "It guarantees freshness to consumers and it keeps dollars in the area. We try to help local family farms succeed by working with them to figure out what's unique to their operation that we can build into our products." For example, some farms can accommodate kosher milk production, which is used in Cedar Grove's line of kosher cheeses. Others have adopted organic practices that support the company's organic products.

"We want to work with farmers who are philosophically aligned with what we're doing. The term 'organic' only goes so far," says Bob. "You can do things like mistreat the cows or treat the workers badly and still meet the minimum requirements for organic." He believes that consumers expect higher standards for organic products, and giving customers what they want has long been one of the company's guiding principles.

In 1993, recognizing that some consumers didn't want dairy products from cows treated with artificial growth hormones (rBGH), Cedar Grove became the first cheese manufacturer in the country to ensure that its products were free of the hormones. Animal enzymes and genetically modified ingredients were also avoided. Cedar Grove accomplished its goal of offering rBGH-free cheese by buying all its milk from local producers who pledged not to treat their cows with synthetic growth hormones.

Today, more than half of Cedar Grove's production is organic, including cheese curds. Cedar Grove also pioneered flavored cheese curds—an idea quickly adopted by competitors. Organic whey powder is another of the company's specialties. Whey is the watery liquid that remains when liquid cheese is heated and separated into curds and whey. Cedar Grove's whey is delivered in 50,000-pound batches to a plant where it's dried into powder and used in organic baked goods, cereals, candy and baby food.

It's easy to be impressed by Cedar Groves' delicious cheese and to admire its community-focused business practices. But a visit to its Living Machine is downright awe inspiring. The only system of its kind used in a cheese factory in the U.S., the trademarked Living Machine is a groundbreaking method for recycling waste water. It looks like a greenhouse bedecked in grapevines, huge tropical plants and potted geraniums. In essence, it functions in the same way as a wetland. Wastewater left behind from the cheesemaking process is funneled through a group of tanks and filters containing plants and microbes and is cleaned so thoroughly that, by the end of the cycle, it can safely flow right back into nearby Honey Creek. A tank of several healthy-looking carp at the end of the line serve as the "canaries in the coal mine," says Bob, ensuring that the system is working properly. In addition to cleaning the water, Living Machine byproducts can be used as fertilizer to support crops or to raise fish.

One of the biggest surprises for Bob was the effect the Living Machine had on the staff. "It's changed the mindset of the employees," he says. "When the water goes down a drain, you don't think about it anymore. But here, if there's a problem with the system, you can see the impacts on the fish and the plants. We waste less product and use less water, which also cuts costs."

Could an operation like Cedar Grove succeed someplace else? "Yes," Bob says immediately. "But it's hard." The current federal pricing system for milk is particularly damaging to smaller businesses and Wisconsin is one of the states hurt the most. The government's system for paying dairy farmers for their milk is riddled with inequities and creates an unfair burden for small producers.

But after so many years at the helm, the best part of the job hasn't changed. For Bob, the most satisfying thing is still "when I take home some cheese and I like it!"

LEADER IN THE INDUSTRY
WISCONSIN SHEEP DAIRY CO-OP, WISCONSIN AND BEYOND

A field full of lambs happily romping about delights the eyes of any passing traveler. The blazing white coats are highlighted against lush green pasture as they prance about. If the capering lambs have the strong genetics of East Friesian or Laucaune breeds, then it's

likely that they'll grow up to move through a dairy parlor and produce rich, creamy sheep milk.

Milking sheep? How is that possible? Although many people in the dairy state are surprised to hear it, sheep dairying is a strong and growing industry in Wisconsin. Although traditional dairy farmers might scratch their heads at the average 300 to 600 pounds per sheep annual milk production (compared to a national average of over 18,000 pounds per dairy cow!), their ears will perk up at the $55 to $60 per hundred pounds farmers are paid for sheep milk, compared to $10 to $15 for conventional cow milk.

Leading the the state in sheep milk production is the Wisconsin Sheep Dairy Cooperative (WSDC), which was incorporated in 1996. "The WSDC basically created an industry in Wisconsin that wasn't here before," states Rich Toebe, the co-op's 2006 president. "A group of farmers have worked together to create this successful business, allowing numerous family farms to be viable." Rich, who is from Catawba, goes on to explain that sheep dairying has drawn a real diversity of farmers. Several members have bought non-working farms and brought them back into operation, others were milking cows and decided to switch to the seasonal sheep system, and others, like Rich himself, were folks from nonfarm backgrounds that chose to begin farming with sheep.

Kim Cassano, Rich's farm partner, adds, "The co-op has had a significant role in growing the sheep dairy industry in the U.S." The Dairy Sheep Association of North America rose out of the membership of the Wisconsin Sheep Dairy Co-op and held its twelfth annual conference in November 2006 in Wisconsin. Institutions like the University of Wisconsin–Extension and the Spooner Research Station have been tremendously helpful, dedicating staff and resources to researching sheep dairy issues. The Spooner Research Station, a member of the co-op, currently milks the largest flock of sheep of the members.

The co-op currently has 12 members with active milking flocks and three additional farms preparing their operations for milking. With an approximate total of 2,500 sheep currently being milked by co-op members, flocks range in size from 60 to over 400 ewes. The WSDC is the only sheep milk co-op in the United States and the largest sheep milk co-op in North America. Although the majority of members live in northwestern Wisconsin, there are also members in Minnesota, Iowa and Nebraska.

Sheep milk may be familiar to consumers as the flavor that brings the spicy bite to a sheep feta or the rich base used in hard Spanish cheeses such as Manchego. It's also the traditional milk used in Italian favorites such as Ricotta and Pecorino Romano as well as French Roquefort cheeses.

WSDC currently ships much of its fresh and frozen sheep's milk to creameries and cheese factories around the country that make it into yogurt and various specialty cheeses. In the past two years, the co-op has developed its own specialty cheeses as well. Co-op members beam when they share that Dante, an aged 100 percent sheep's milk cheese, won top honors in its class in the 2006 American Cheese Society competition. Mona, a 50 percent sheep's milk and 50 percent cow's milk cheese, is also extremely well regarded nationally. The co-op has recently begun producing a 100 percent sheep feta and is now distributing its cheeses at finer shops and restaurants coast to coast.

"Our cheeses are made at small Wisconsin cheese factories where they are produced in small batches and given great attention," Rich notes. "The cheesemakers practice 'affinage,' which is the art of aging the cheese—turning, washing and salting. The very special process of caring for the ripening cheese is one of the things that makes our cheeses unique."

GOOD ENOUGH TO EAT

Kim adds, "Cheesemakers enjoy working with sheep milk, as it has very complex flavors. It is creamier, has the most well-developed flavors of the big three milks (sheep, goat, cow) and has a higher yield of cheese per pound of milk." Sheep milk is also unique in that it can be frozen and then thawed for cheese production. The milk is naturally homogenized—fat particles are bonded to proteins so there is no "cream line"—and freezing does not adversely affect the qualities that are important for cheesemaking. This is a huge marketing advantage over other types of milk, as the window of freshness can be expanded by several months. The co-op does, however, have a fresh milk pickup route, as producing fresh milk is a lot easier and less labor and cost intensive for the farmers.

At Jump River Shepherd's Dairy, Rich and Kim manage their flock of 150 milking sheep and the lambs and dry ewes on rotationally grazed pasture. A majority of the co-op's members have their sheep out on pasture for most of the growing season. This allows them to take advantage of the rich vitamins, minerals and other qualities the grass diet adds to the milk and, ultimately, to the cheeses. "Sheep dairying is naturally seasonal," Rich notes. "The sheep usually have lambs in the spring, and we'll milk for about eight months during the best pasture season." The ability to freeze milk means that even though most of the milk is produced seasonally, milk sales and cheese production can be year-round. Some co-op members have been moving to breed their sheep out of the typical season, to increase the availability of fresh milk year-round.

Recruitment materials distributed by the co-op make it clear that sheep dairying isn't for everyone. Hard physical work is required. Even though sheep are smaller than cows, they are strong! In addition, long hours are unavoidable at certain times of the year. Helping in the lambing shed with 200 expectant ewes is a multi-week, round-the-clock proposition. These arduous demands will weed out those who think milking sheep represents the easy life. Sheep, however, are engaging creatures (much smarter than their

reputation indicates) and co-op members as a whole enjoy the challenges of working with the relatively docile animals. Many members do not farm full-time, although Rich and Kim, and a few other families, are able to fully support themselves as sheep dairy farmers.

As the only major producer of Grade A (fluid) sheep milk in the U.S., the WSDC is having a significant impact on the Wisconsin economy. Rich says, "With the cheese plants, feed mills, agricultural supply, lamb sales and transportation support, the co-op impacts a lot of jobs and contributes a lot of dollars."

At this stage the cooperative has no regularly paid employees. All of the work to manage the milk collection, testing and quality control, financial management, cheese production and the marketing of both raw and finished products is done by co-op members. Choosing to market as a group has real advantages but comes at a price in terms of organizational development and time spent to support the good of all the members. The co-op is still young and hopes, eventually, to grow large enough to support a management staff.

Looking ahead, Rich summarizes the co-op's goals: to continue expanding the branded cheese line; to continue producing high quality sheep milk for those who buy raw milk; and to grow the number of farmers the Co-op supports. "We are trying to provide a way for sustainable family farms to continue being successful and provide opportunities for new farmers," Rich concludes. With overall production growth of 25 to 30 percent, it's clear that the Wisconsin Sheep Dairy co-op has excelled at developing this new industry, benefiting farmers and communities alike. Plus they have created delicious sheep cheeses that are now available to customers countrywide.

THE FRUITS AND HONEY OF THEIR LABOR

White Winter Winery, Iron River

The large fermenting drum hisses as Jon Hamilton removes the lid. Inside is a deep purplish liquid. As you lean in, a plethora of smells rush upwards—rich tangy fruits and berries and the subtlest of sweet scents. Your nose is your best tool, Jon explains, as he peers into a drum of what will soon be mead—an ancient drink, as old as the Vikings who consumed it. Jon and his wife, Kim, opened White Winter Winery in Iron River, located along U.S. Highway 2 in northern Wisconsin, in 1996. They are one of only a few mead makers in the country, relying on traditions as old as time to create the unique brew. They use locally produced honey and fruit, making truly regional beverages.

In the ten years since the business started, Jon and Kim have watched it grow from a basement business to a full-blown enterprise. Honey is where it all began. Jon's family kept bees for generations; but without growing to a commercial size, one cannot survive on honey sales alone. So, after attending Northland College in Ashland—where Jon met Kim—the two decided to take their degrees in psychology and education and pursue mead production as their entrepreneurial goal. They began with a two-year tour around the country for research and development. They wanted to see what people had done, learn from their trials and tribulations, and really figure out whether their dream was a possibility.

The original location of the winery is two blocks east from where it is now. With a small shop upstairs, they had produced the mead in a cramped basement. With a 5 to 20 percent annual increase in sales in their first eight years, they finally outgrew their original space and moved into a new building.

The new location of White Winter Winery has a story all its own. Originally the Bayfield Electrical Co-op, the structure was moved so a new foundation slab could be laid down and the building moved back on top of it. The interior was restored and refinished by Clancy Ward, a local timber frame carpenter, who used local hardwoods to beautify the retail area of the winery. The new production room contains two 500-gallon and two 1,000-gallon dairy tanks, once used by Wisconsin farmers for storing milk.

In their new facility, Jon and Kim can make an estimated 10,000 to 15,000 gallons of mead per year, up from the 3,000 to 5,000 gallon capacity of their former location. In addition to traditional

mead, the Hamiltons make Melomel, which incorporates fruit at the time of fermentation, Cyser, made from fresh pressed apple cider and Bracket, which is made from honey and grain. In addition to these tasty treats, the Hamiltons also produce hard apple cider and pear cider as well as two non-alcoholic drinks. With continued interest in their products, Jon anticipates another 10 to 20 percent increase in production over the next three years.

Given the quantities of honey they need, the Hamiltons had to supplant the honey produced by their bees with that purchased from local farmers. Jon and Kim buy approximately 25 to 30 thousand pounds of honey and fruit a year from farmers within a 150-mile radius of their business. Local farmers, in fact, propelled the Hamilton's operation. For several years, Highland Valley Farm donated hundreds of pounds of blueberries to the winery, which Jon used to experiment on different beverages.

"The learning curve has been nearly vertical for me," Jon says. From early on, Jon and Kim's sense of sustainability and community began where they left off: college. They sought the help of Rick Dowd, a chemistry professor at Northland College, their alma mater. "We bartered," says Jon. "I gave him honey and he reviewed my acid titration techniques to ensure that the processes that took place were correct."

Local brewers aided in product development, and countless local farmers quickly demonstrated trust in their business relationships. The Hamiltons made their business public-private in 2001, welcoming new people interested in becoming shareholders.

"What's good for me is what's good for the next guy," says Jon. "What goes around comes around.... You help people out and they help you out."

WHERE THE PIGS RUN AND PLAY FREELY

Willow Creek Farm, Loganville

Every aspect of life on Willow Creek Farm connects through a common theme: quality. Nestled amongst the lush green slopes of the Baraboo Hills in central Wisconsin, the Renger family handle every aspect of their hog operation with a commitment to providing their animals with the best care and to producing premium meats.

Top Madison chefs laud the distinct quality of Willow Creek Farm meats. Loyal customer demand keeps the business growing and profitable. "We moved to Wisconsin with the desire to create a business that would enable us to live where we wanted to be and provide a strong quality of life for our family. The pigs sure have delivered on this," smiles Tony Renger, who runs Willow Creek Farm along with his partner and wife, Sue, with help from their three children.

Tony brought fourth-generation Iowa family farming roots to Willow Creek Farm while Sue came with her Polish grandfather's kielbasa recipe. After moving to their current house and ten acres in 1993, Tony and Sue used the next eight years to purchase more land. Eighty acres and three children later, the hard-working couple officially started raising hogs in 2001. Tony racked up a range of experiences before choosing to return to farming, from corporate stints to working at both confinement factory farms and pasture-based operations. "I've seen both sides of raising livestock and there was no question as to how we wanted to farm, providing a healthy, humane environment for the animals and thereby also for ourselves," explains Tony. "In many ways, we're raising hogs in a

similar manner to how my parents and grandparents ran the farm, with a foremost commitment to providing a strong quality of life for the animals."

Farming proved to be a new experience for Sue, having grown up in the Detroit area. "When you grow up in the city, you go to the store and you buy your shrink-wrapped meat and you have no connection to where this animal came from, what type of life it had and how it was treated. This has been a whole new journey for me as I've experienced the whole other side of where our food comes from," Sue notes.

Now raising about 400 head a year, Tony and Sue only rear purebred Berkshire hogs, an English breed renowned for its quality and taste. They take their hogs to a local processor every Tuesday, selling their meat cuts as well as sausages to a local southwestern Wisconsin market. Willow Creek Farm sales split about equally between restaurants, including Madison's local food leaders L'Etoile and Lombardino's, Madison retail outlets such as Willy Street Co-op, and direct sales to customers, primarily through their booth at the Dane County Farmers' Market.

Willow Creek Farm's commitment to the humane treatment of their pigs earned them the distinction of being the first individual, family-run pig farm approved by the Animal Welfare Institute (AWI), a nonprofit organization dedicated to promoting humane farming practices and halting the growth of factory farming. At Willow Creek

Farm, sows build natural nests and live in social groups. There's no continuous confinement of the animals or removal of pig tails, and no routine use of antibiotics. "At our farm, pigs not only play, they can run around smelling and exploring their surroundings," explains Tony. Additionally, Tony and Sue grow their own feed corn using a non-GMO corn that yields a high-oil kernel. This corn's improved palatability is especially good for pigs, as it gives the animals more energy. Learning through trial and error with their Berkshire pigs, Tony grinds soybeans and other grains to ensure a fresh, high-quality feed ration providing balanced essential minerals and oils at each phase of a pig's development.

Happy, healthy hogs result in superior-tasting meat, evidenced in the letters of praise from loyal customers hanging on the walls of the modest, on-site office. "The French have a term called '*terroir*,' meaning that a food's flavor stems from the sense of place and geography of where it was grown or raised," Tony explains. "We like to think one can taste the terroir in our pork, tasting the flavors of the farm's landscape where the pigs play, run and graze." With the exception of Sue's grandfather's authentic Polish kielbasa recipe, the Rengers have developed all of their own recipes for items such as brats and Andouille sausage, purchasing high-quality organic spices from Frontier Natural Products Co-op in Iowa.

With a denser meat, the Berkshire product retains moisture better and does not dry out when cooking, resulting in a darker color. "I have to laugh when conventional pork producers talk about pork as 'the other white meat,' because it really isn't and shouldn't be," says Sue. "We spend a lot of time on education, particularly when we're at the farmers' market, to help reeducate folks about what meat should taste and look like. So often today, people are far removed from where their meat comes from."

Thanks to Sue and Tony's leadership and education efforts, consumer interest in buying local, sustainably grown food direct from the grower continues to swell. "More and more, people want to know how their food was made and where it came from," Sue comments. The Renger's reputation earned them the opportunity to travel and speak on behalf of humane animal treatment. The Madison chapter of Slow Food, an international organization dedicated to promoting local, sustainable foods, asked the Rengers to represent the area's sustainable meat growers at the Terra Madre World Meeting of Food Communities in Turin, Italy. Most recently, the Animal Welfare Institute invited Sue and Tony to present at the Eursafe Conference in Norway, helping establish Wisconsin as a leader in the sustainable foods movement. Additionally, they presented testimony to Congress in coalition with other animal welfare groups, promoting the welfare of animals. "Interest in these topics continues to skyrocket," Sue notes. "There was standing room only when our groups presented testimony."

Such demand enables the Rengers to not only continue to expand Willow Creek Farm but to do so in a thoughtful, community-based manner. Willow Creek recently contracted with three other local farms to raise Berkshire feeder pigs for them. Sue and Tony purchase these piglets at around nine to eleven weeks and then raise them until they're fully grown. As the youngest of their three children enters school next year, the Rengers look to having more time in the near future to work on fine-tuning their business.

"Our hogs garner a premium retail price compared to what we would receive from the traditional commodities market, but we do have higher costs," explains Tony. "Sure, we could save some pennies by buying cheaper spices or using a lesser grade meat processor, but these ingredients all collectively add up to create the distinct Willow Creek Farm flavors that keeps our customers loyal."

BEER WITH A HOME
VIKING BREWING COMPANY, DALLAS

Marry a nuclear physicist with Norwegian ancestors to a technical writer from Swedish stock, settle them deep in the country, and what do you get? Great beer!

Of course the real story is not quite that simple, but there's no doubt about the simple success of Randy and Ann Lee's Viking Brewing Company, named for their Scandinavian ancestors and headquartered in the tiny town of Dallas in western Wisconsin. Behind the microbrewery's 20-plus unique beers (available in select stores and taverns in Wisconsin and Minnesota) lies a deep commitment to craftsmanship and the Lees' determination to find a way to make a living and a life in the rural surroundings of their childhoods. Beer names like "Dim Whit," "Queen Victoria's Secret," "Big Swede" and "Abby Normal" make it clear that the two also mix a funky approach and an offbeat sense of humor with their brewing enterprise.

Since 1995, when the Lees bought the old 20,000 square-foot Dallas Creamery where Randy's grandfather used to work, Viking Brewing has seen steady growth. Since 2004, they've been brewing at their capacity of three hundred 31-gallon barrels per year. "Something has really changed since we started," Randy says.

"Back then it was 'micro-what?' Now the traditional beer market is falling, and the microbrewery market is taking off."

In contrast to the conventional wisdom that has made bland beer ubiquitous in the U.S., Viking Brewing isn't afraid to put some big flavors in their beers. "There's a lot of women who go for the heavy, dark brews. Maybe women have better taste buds," Randy laughs. Beer lovers these days are more willing to expand their horizons, Ann adds. "Now the attitude is, 'what do you have that's new?'" A good question. The Lees offer four year-round beers, including "Copperhead," their best-selling brew, and a changing palette of seasonal beers. "Like this one—'Morketid.' It means 'dark time' in Norwegian; it's a winter beer," Ann says. "Then there are beers to look forward to in the spring—'Sylvan Springs;' and summer—'Lime Twist.' And we've got a traditional spiced Christmas beer."

Other beers are brewed to fill in gaps in the color range (from light to dark), add a new style (like Belgian beer), or just to see if an idea will work (as with chocolate pepper beer). "Usually we come up with ideas for a new beer together or sometimes one of us has an inspiration," Randy laughs. "With Dim Whit, we had the name before the beer," Ann adds. "You've got to have a sense of humor."

The two also have a sense of history and respect for the craft of brewing. The art of beer making reaches back many centuries in many countries and encompasses a bewildering array of production styles. The Lees take the approach of creating a full palette of beers brewed with traditional ingredients and methods but add their own Wisconsin twist. A different strain of yeast is used for each brew, and the beers are not pasteurized. "Our beer is alive, it changes. It really needs to be kept cool," Ann notes. "Pasteurization is really, really bad for beer."

Besides marketing through regional distributors, the Lees maintain a full schedule of beer shows, community festivals, fundraisers and brew fests through the year, traveling as far as Madison and the Twin Cities. The motivation is partly marketing and partly getting together with other brewers and beer lovers. "We've met so many fabulous people along the way," Ann says. "In most businesses there's intense competition," Randy adds. "In this business, at the brewers' level, there's an incredible amount of camaraderie."

Community, whether it's business peers or neighbors, is at the heart of why the Lees chose to center their lives in a small rural town. "We view ourselves as a cog in our favorite community," Randy comments, adding that they want to contribute to "a rebirth of the rural economy." "I did the Milwaukee thing, the Fargo thing, and it's not healthy," Ann adds. "My new slogan is to think locally, not globally. Community is so important. Community is how we're going to survive. Get out there and lend a hand."

She's setting a good example of how to do just that. As a member of the Dallas Civic Club, Ann heard old-time residents' stories of how free movies used to be shown in the town park on Friday nights and decided to resurrect that tradition. "It's been a huge hit. We had a 'Popeye' night, we show old 'Ma and Pa Kettle' movies," she smiles. Families bring lawn chairs, the club sells popcorn and pop, and the town has a place to gather on warm summer evenings.

Ann also sits on the board of the *Hay River Review*, the area newspaper, and single-handedly began the annual Dallas Oktoberfest, which not only features Viking Brews, a pancake breakfast and an arts and crafts fair, but also "guns, live steel combat, and polka music. Ah... Wisconsin!" according to the promotional fliers.

Randy, who works full-time in Eau Claire in addition to being the brewery technician, has found time to sit on the township's Land Use Plan Commission. He also found time, in 2002, to run for governor. The whole thing was Ann's idea. "I said I'm going to have you run for governor," she says. "I just put it on our web site." Randy's candidacy on the BEER party platform—for Balance, Education, Environment, Reform—was featured on the front pages of both the Rice Lake and Eau Claire papers, and he even got some votes that fall. "We were 90 percent kidding," Randy notes. "But that other 10 percent..."

While the Lees acknowledge that their community orientation and dedication to an artisan product can't compete with corporate America, they believe they don't have to compete. They are on the verge of expanding production to 3,000 barrels a year, which should allow Randy to work full-time with Ann at the brewery. "We have to get bigger, just for the economics," he says. But by staying with a high-end, regional product, Viking avoids competing with national brands. "It's like dancing with elephants. You have to watch where they're stepping and get out of the way," Randy adds. "The last thing we need is to get in a price war with somebody."

Though Randy and Ann's "ongoing conversation," as they call it, with the craft of brewing, local food systems and rural society still has a long way to go, they know they've already accomplished the most important thing. "Dare I say happiness?" Ann concludes. "Randy, are you happy?"

He smiles, "Oh, yeah."

THE NATURAL CHOICE IN AGRICULTURE

CRYSTAL CREEK, TREGO

When opening the door to an unassuming warehouse in a quiet tree-thickened setting just north of Trego, one doesn't expect the flurry of activity inside. With phone lines buzzing and wheeled carts of product zipping by, it is obvious one has stepped into the realm of a dynamic business. Here is Crystal Creek, a thriving family-owned business that provides livestock farmers with quality natural supplements and nutritional programs.

Started in 1996 by Dan Leiterman and his wife, Jan, Crystal Creek, a division of Leiterman and Associates, Inc., was a brainstorm in response to a need Dan noticed in his work as a livestock nutritionist. "I bumped into organic farmers in 1995 and became fascinated with their philosophies on utilizing the circle of life: producing quality feed to promote animal health," Dan remembers. "After an intensive learning process, I felt a drive to help people improve their livestock nutrition through organic and sustainable methods." Dan found that organic and sustainable farmers were limited by a lack of information as well as appropriate materials to help maintain their animals' health. He realized that with his 23-year background as a nutritionist and agronomist, he could do something to help these farmers, and Crystal Creek was formed.

Crystal Creek started in Leiterman's home garage in Prescott, with the help of Jan and their two sons, as a sideline to Dan's consulting business. Recognizing it was critical that the family keep a high quality of life while developing the business, the Leitermans moved north to rural Trego in 2001 where their outdoor hobbies, which include working with their sled dogs, hiking and fishing, are readily accessible. "We decided to move to Trego to keep up our essential connection with nature," Dan smiles. "We like it because it's nice and quiet." To better serve their customers, Dan and Jan are opening a new facility in Spooner, 15 miles from their home.

The business's mission statement says: "Crystal Creek is dedicated to providing livestock producers with the very best natural, effective and environmentally safe livestock supplements and programs possible." Dan is a firm believer in the use of science-based research to drive the development of Crystal Creek products. He explains, "I hear a need expressed by producers for a solution to a particular problem. I do a data search of international research to find possible solutions. I then use my experience as a nutritionist to put together a logical formulation, which is then tested on volunteer herds to verify performance." Many cultures around the world have large knowledge banks with extremely credible research relevant to sustainable livestock production. Dan explores this research to lead him to effective formulations. Crystal Creek's extensive testing of formulations assures effectiveness before a product graduates into permanent product status.

Although most of their products are allowed in certified organic production systems, Dan has noticed that many of their clients are not organic and that a growing number of traditional veterinarians are recommending Crystal Creek products. "Farmers are frustrated and find that their conventional treatments aren't working. They want to see healthy animals and are recognizing that immune system support and improving basic nutrition will help them thrive," Dan notes. He believes that farmers need to learn nutrition on a deeper level and get more proactive with nutrition to support livestock health. "Farmers need to support optimum animal performance so that they don't get backed into a corner where it is easy to reach for antibiotics and hormones."

The beautiful Crystal Creek catalog offers nutrition and health products for dairy and beef cows, horses, poultry, sheep, goats and swine. With product names such as "Bright Start," "Freedom Flour" and "Udder Fancy," it isn't hard to imagine the products will have a positive impact. The "Crystal Creek Pantry" also offers several products for human health. Base materials for Crystal Creek products include botanicals, minerals, trace elements, yeasts, microbials and other natural ingredients and are available in several formulations, including boluses (rather intimidating giant gel capsules), powders, pellets, tinctures, lotions and liquids. The catalog is rich with details on product ingredient lists, use instructions and overviews of the basics of livestock nutrition.

"Our advertising has been limited and we haven't had salesmen," says Dan. "The majority of our growth has come from word-of-mouth recommendations." With strong growth every year, the business's low-key marketing strategy has served them well. Crystal Creek currently has ten employees and works directly with thousands of farmers and more than 65 dealers (feed mills and veterinarians) around the U.S.

The business is based on mail order and LTL (less than truck load) trucking delivery, with warehouse operations and staff currently housed in Trego. "We have a positive impact on the local economy," Dan observes. Located just north of this small, unincorporated community, Crystal Creek hires locally and offers well-paying jobs. "We have recently been adding two to three employees a year, and I expect that trend to continue," says Dan.

There is a licensed veterinarian on staff to assist in verifying product function and to help consult with clients. "Training farmers about livestock nutrition and health is key to their and our success," Dan notes. "We regularly get calls from dealers or groups of farmers to come out and do workshops." The company offers a regular informational newsletter to their customers and a website rich with articles and notes on specific health concerns and nutritional suggestions. Future plans include space at the new Crystal Creek facility to conduct livestock nutrition training.

Dan and staff have also recently re-expanded into nutritional consulting. "I love it," Dan exclaims. "Consulting with individual farms on feed rations can take a lot of time, but in order to properly support optimum livestock health, you need to start with the basic feed ration. It only makes sense for Crystal Creek to offer this assistance."

"Our products are not a silver bullet," Dan concludes. "My primary interest is in helping people to better understand livestock nutrition so that the health of animals is better supported and the need for antibiotics and drugs is reduced." He continues, "What I find exciting about agriculture today is that farmers can appreciate the best of the best—they have stepped back into the circle of life and are finding they can be successful and still be in tune with Mother Nature." Crystal Creek is itself certainly connected with nature, and is a business that reflects the values it advocates.

GOOD ENOUGH TO EAT

LEARNING & ACTION

Learning doesn't start, or stop, at the entrance to a campus or at the doorstep of a limestone building. Spread across Wisconsin are a wealth of organizations that provide information and training to people looking for something a little bit different.

In the stories shared here, learning flourishes in greenhouses and urban gardens. Educators share their messages under big tents in the blaze of a summer day, at a conference center in the middle of winter or at a lively community fair. Youth are empowered.

Sustainable farmers are grown. Food systems are better understood. And energy solutions are adopted.

Our stories of educators show a broad commitment to providing information and knowledge in ways that are hands-on, accessible, inspiring and life-changing. Not to mention fun! The organizations we highlight possess many gifts in inspiring and developing those who will be the heart of the renewal of the Wisconsin countryside!

"FARMING CAN CHANGE THEIR LIVES"
GROWING POWER, MILWAUKEE

On a modest piece of land on Milwaukee's northwest side, Will Allen is growing Milwaukee's future. Will is the co-director of Growing Power and has spent more than ten years showing children, particularly poor city kids, that farming can change their lives.

Children like Anthony Jackson. Anthony first came to the Growing Power site when he was 13 years old to earn money for school clothes through a work program organized by his church. Now 27 and married, Anthony is on Growing Power's board of directors and hopes to one day have his own piece of land to farm. "It started out just as a job," says Anthony. "But I fell in love with the place and with farming. It's really kind of amazing what it does to you."

Amazing is one word to describe the living landscape that Will runs out of six unassuming greenhouses on two acres in urban Milwaukee. As grocery stores and farmers' markets have moved out of urban areas, replaced by convenience stores and fast food restaurants, the distance between people and the land on which their food is grown has increased. Growing Power has stepped in to close this gap by providing fresh produce to people who might not otherwise have access to healthy food in Milwaukee, Chicago and other communities in the region served by the SHARE (Self Help And Resource Exchange) Food Network. Set among apartments, ranch homes and an Army reserve training base, the nonprofit Growing Power turns out more than two million pounds of food a year.

Producing food is only one of Growing Power's community-driven programs, however. The organization also offers training through on-site, hands-on workshops held year-round, and provides networking opportunities that involve everything from helping farmers find markets to helping communities convert vacant or degraded land to productive gardens. Thousands of people, including school kids, tour the facility each year, purchase food in the retail store and participate in classes. Although Growing Power is involved in more than 60 different programs and projects, food remains at the heart of the organization and at the heart of the man behind it all.

Growing up on a rural Maryland farm, Will learned early on the value of hard work and good food. "Food has been at the center of my existence as far back as I can remember," he says. "Growing food taught me to never give up when things got tough."

Will's hard work resulted in a basketball scholarship and he became a star player at the University of Miami. He then spent several years playing professional ball for the American Basketball Association and for several European teams. Hanging up his sneakers in 1976, Will and his family returned to Oak Creek, Wisconsin, where his wife's family operated a farm and where he took a job in marketing for Proctor and Gamble. But a few years in the corporate world left Will wanting something more—something he could only find working the land.

So he gave up his suit and tie and returned to farming full-time in Oak Creek. Driving down Silver Springs Drive one day, he spotted the Growing Power site—the last working farm in Milwaukee—and purchased the land as a place to sell organic produce from his Oak

Creek farm. Eventually, this little piece of land began turning out crops of its own.

In 1995, Will met some kids from a local YMCA who wanted to start a garden to sell produce at a neighborhood market. He got them space to sell at the market and offered to help them with their garden. But when he saw the two small, weedy plots of land the kids intended to use, he offered them space behind his greenhouses and a hands-on lesson in growing food.

Throughout the rest of the summer, the kids came out three times a week to work in the garden in addition to spending Saturdays at the market. It was a long hot summer and Will thought the kids would quit after a few days. But they didn't. When groundhogs ate the

kids' beans and cabbage, he thought that this time, the kids would quit for sure. But they didn't. "They really hung in there despite all the challenges," says Will, laughing. "Those kids really impressed me and really inspired me to continue to try to get kids involved in growing food and farming."

Soon after, Will organized the nonprofit Farm City Link, a forerunner to Growing Power, to teach children to garden. In 1998, Will met Hope Finkelstein, who had formed Growing Power to bring together all the food and farm assistance programs in the Madison area. The two soon agreed to merge operations under the Growing Power name, which allowed Will to devote his energy to teaching while Hope managed the organization's administration.

Growing Power offers many kids their only chance to get down into the dirt and to get up close and personal with their food. Working the soil changes kids, says Will. They learn to appreciate the soil and the difficulties as well as the rewards of farming. "Kids can come here to get hands-on experience and make connections that they will never get growing beans in a Styrofoam cup," he says. "They do so much better if they can get involved and there isn't anything here that kids aren't involved in."

More than 30 different schools and community groups come to play in Will's soil each year. Many keep coming back. Students from Milwaukee schools work as interns where they learn composting, vermiculture, beekeeping, aquaculture and more. Twelve students are enrolled in the Youth Corps, a multiyear apprenticeship program that trains underprivileged kids in elementary school through college in all aspects of the growing and selling operation.

Anthony recalls becoming a manager of Growing Power's retail store by age 16. "Will made us feel so respected and special," he says. "There was nothing we did that Will wouldn't do. We were all equals there and it taught me the value of hard, really hard, work." Many of these kids first learn about Growing Power through visits to the retail store with their parents. In addition to work at the main Growing Power site itself, members of the Youth Corps take field trips to other farms, assist with workshops and conferences and help with planting and harvesting at the Boys' and Girls' Club camp in Waukesha County. Will has also hired a teacher from Milwaukee Public Schools to teach reading and writing lessons as a corollary to the hands-on farming. A few former Youth Corps members have even gone on to work for Growing Power. And Growing Power also helped Anthony pay for college.

Will is constantly surprised by how hard kids can and are willing to work. "Kids give adults so much energy," he says. "They learn much faster than adults too. People think that inner-city kids wouldn't like farming, but that idea flies out the door the first time they dig their hands into the soil and really feel the earth."

Changing lives and eating habits takes time, but Will has committed himself to the long haul. He envisions the organization expanding across the country so that more communities have access to safe and healthy food, and more urban kids have the opportunity to learn life skills, farming expertise and community responsibility. Growing Power has already extended its work to Chicago, where Will's daughter, Erika, manages its programs.

"The transformation doesn't happen overnight, but I know it can happen because I have seen it with my own eyes, so we go all the way," Will says. "Food brings people together. It transcends poverty and is at the forefront of community development and sustainability. Food is wealth, wealth that must be shared with future generations."

AT MOSES WE GROW FARMERS
MIDWEST ORGANIC AND SUSTAINABLE EDUCATION SERVICE, SPRING VALLEY

The motto of the Midwest Organic and Sustainable Education Service (MOSES) is bold: "At MOSES, We Grow Farmers." Bold, yes, but MOSES is true to its motto.

Take, for example, organic vegetable farmer Chris Blanchard. Chris recalls when MOSES first came into his life several years ago. "Kim and I were getting ready to move back to the Midwest to farm, and called around looking for resources," he says. "Everyone said we should call Faye Jones (MOSES's executive director), and even though she was in the middle of her busy farming season, she took the time to talk to me—a farmer from Maine. She looked up phone numbers, made recommendations about potential markets and where we may find the kind of farm we were looking for. And that is what MOSES is still really all about—connecting people and resources."

Chris notes that this "role as connector" is what farmers really look for and value in MOSES. Although written resources are available, it is the personal touch that is most appreciated. "MOSES doesn't just send you a pile of written material," Chris explains, "they try to find the answer to your question, or connect you to someone that knows."

Faye has been leading MOSES since its inception in 1999. Initially, she was the coordinator of the now famous Upper

Midwest Organic Farming Conference held in La Crosse each February. In recent years the conference has drawn more than 2,300 attendees, coming from all over the country. As the conference grew, the developing need for improved resources and education to help those interested in organic production became apparent. "Organic farming is complex," Faye notes. "Organic farmers have traditionally learned from each other, but it became clear that there were other resources that were also needed."

And so MOSES was born, with a mission to "help agriculture make the transition to a sustainable organic system of farming that is ecologically sound, economically viable and socially just, through information, education, research and integrating the broader community into this effort." This mission has led the organization into several projects with broad impacts. Faye, her staff and a nine-member board of directors, the majority of whom are farmers, design and fund numerous activities in the seven Midwestern states that MOSES claims as its territory.

It is not by coincidence that the MOSES' office is located in Wisconsin. Organic farming is very important in the state, so much so that the governor has made a commitment to encourage its growth. Currently, Wisconsin is second only to California in the number of organic farms, and top in the country for number of organic dairy cows!

Overall demand in the U.S. for organic products has grown over 20 percent annually for more than 20 years. As a result, organic agriculture is one of the fastest growing sectors in agriculture today. The demand for many organic products currently outstrips supply, and there is a need for more farmers to take on organic production. Farmers turn to MOSES for help in understanding successful organic practices and the laws governing organic production and marketing. "MOSES is here to provide tools and resources to improve the

understanding of organic farming," Faye reflects. "Our goal is to create more sustainable and organic farmers."

MOSES currently operates with a staff of five full-time and two part-time people plus a few regular contractors who work on special projects. "Our budget and staff have doubled in less than three years. We have really stepped up our ability to provide services and information to help farmers," Faye notes with pride.

Projects range from the high-profile Upper Midwest Organic Farming Conference to a diversity of written publications, an information-rich website, in-person trainings and a new organic farmer hotline. The annual conference offers an opportunity for farmers, educators, Extension agents, bankers, students and others to gather together in a fun environment to learn best practices from each other. Many attendees treat the conference weekend as an important mini-vacation: a time to eat well, enjoy lots of great conversation and fill their brains with useful information.

One new initiative, entitled "Help Wanted: Organic Farmers," is directly aimed at growing more organic farmers. The initiative not only offers workshops about organic production and certification to farmers around the state, but it also connects farmers directly to MOSES' organic outreach specialist, Harriet Behar, via a toll-free organic farmers' hotline. Harriet provides quick and complete customized answers to organic production and certification questions. Hundreds of callers have appreciated having someone who knows how to navigate the maze of regulations and paperwork of organic certification outlined by the USDA (U.S. Department of Agriculture) organic law. "Farmers are incredibly relieved to have a real person offering help," Harriet claims.

Meanwhile, Chris sums up his thoughts about the vibrant educational organization: "Organic farming is all about

relationships—the relationship between different microbes in the soil, between plants and the microbes, and between the soil and plants and animals. Organic farming has a critical relationship to the economic health of the countryside. And organic farming is rich with relationships among the farmers who have adopted organic systems. MOSES plants seeds for relationships, and then helps those germinate and grow."

As one of the farmers that MOSES has helped grow, Chris so believes in the mission of MOSES that he went on to join the board of directors and has been an active organizer for the Upper Midwest Organic Farming Conference for the last eight years.

MOSES fosters relationships, and ultimately that is what grows more farmers. "At MOSES, We Grow Farmers!"

EMPOWERING AN ENERGY REVOLUTION
MIDWEST RENEWABLE ENERGY ASSOCIATION, CUSTER

A powerful new vision for a more sustainable world based upon energy efficiency, conservation, renewable energy and sustainable living is energizing the Midwest. The Midwest Renewable Energy Association (MREA) combines this vision of its forward-thinking founders with the swelling ranks of mostly rural landowners to create the world's largest and longest-running Renewable Energy and Sustainable Living Fair. The MREA provides the educational resources and shares the know-how that's transforming the Midwest—if not also the nation—into more self-reliant, ecologically responsible and economically thriving local communities. The 3,000-plus member nonprofit organization based in rural Custer is serving as the epicenter for explosive growth in the renewable energy industry and related sustainable living businesses, including green design and construction, natural building and energy efficiency.

What happened to those energy fairs of the late 1970s? This question, raised in 1989 by Richard Perez, publisher of *Home Power* magazine, ended up serving as a catalyst for the first Wisconsin-based energy fair held in August of 1990. The effort was led by a group of mostly local back-to-the-land types—many having graduated from the University of Wisconsin-Stevens Point with a strong commitment to environmental education—who decided to create an event akin to those old energy fairs. What they didn't realize is that it would change the course of renewable energy development in the Midwest, bring thousands of rural residents into the fold of more self-reliant and sustainable living, jumpstart the

adoption of new renewable energy systems, foster the creation of hundreds of small businesses related to sustainable living and improve the quality of life for anyone living, working or playing in the region's countryside.

"We were an action-oriented, community-based group of homesteaders with an environmental bent, often living out of VW vans with everything plugged into a cigarette lighter, powered by a solar electric module on the roof," chuckles Mick Sagrillo, one of the MREA's founders and its current president. "Everything clicked for our first energy fair with workshops based on the premise that education is empowerment. We featured the most democratic of natural resources, wind and sun, since just about anyone could produce their own power."

Despite its apparent middle-of-nowhere location at the Portage County fairgrounds outside Amherst, the event achieved unprecedented national media coverage. This was due, in large part, to the U.S. invasion of Iraq that happened just two weeks before the fair's opening. "We suddenly had interest in how renewable energy and energy conservation could provide homegrown solutions to the U.S. dependency on overseas oil and related political instability," Mick explains. "The fair was another option that many homeowners and businesses were eager to explore. The more you know in order to meet your energy needs, the less you need to pay." A rainy downpour and muddied fairgrounds threatened to undermine this first energy fair, which was mostly funded by penny change cobbled together by its hard-working volunteer organizers. But, once the weather cleared up, over 4,000 people attended.

About a year later, the MREA received its nonprofit status as an organization dedicated to promoting renewable energy, energy efficiency and sustainable living through education and demonstration. Besides hosting the Renewable Energy and Sustainable Living Fair every year, today the MREA offers hands-on workshops year-round for individuals and businesses to gain the skill sets needed to install their own systems. Workshops include how to diversify an existing business into one of the fast-growing niche areas of renewable energy system design, site analysis, installation and maintenance and natural building.

As a part of this educational effort, the MREA certifies renewable energy site assessors for wind, solar electric and solar thermal systems. "Suddenly, rural electricians, small engineering firms and contractors were forming their own companies and going out on their own to educate homeowners or businesses about how to put together a renewable energy system to meet their needs," says Clay Sterling, the MREA's education director. "This certification is a way for customers to ensure that their system is installed by someone with solid training."

The ReNew the Earth Institute—a building that serves as a one-stop eco-demonstration facility—along with a website and membership newsletter add to the reach and impact. The ReNew the Earth Institute is a state-of-the-art demonstration eco-office complex, retrofitted from an existing building. A solar thermal system provides in-floor radiant heat for a classroom and two wind turbine systems and several solar electric systems generate over 7,000 kilowatts of electricity annually to power the facility. The 4,200-square-foot structure houses the MREA staff, which includes eight full-time and one part-time employees, and showcases hands-on educational displays, leading conservation and efficiency products and numerous examples of other natural building materials. The training facility, which is accredited by the Institute of Sustainable Power, is surrounded by spectacular perennial demonstration gardens and the wind and solar electric systems that power it.

Today, over 20,000 people—from farmers to rural business owners, from school teachers to elected officials—descend on Custer for the fair during the third weekend in June, attending over 125 workshops facilitated by leading experts in their field and participating in working demonstrations of energy efficient technologies and renewable energy systems. Featuring more than 225 exhibitor booths staffed by experts from companies showcasing their award-winning renewable energy systems, energy efficient products or sustainable services, as well as leading nonprofit organizations, the exhibitor area is a one-stop shop for anyone thinking about making a change to renewable energy or a more sustainable approach to living or working.

A special exhibitor dinner prior to the opening of the fair fosters business-to-business collaboration and networking that continues throughout the three-day event.

"The fair attracts movers and shakers from across the nation to present workshops that address wind, solar electric, solar thermal, natural or green buildings, and many other topics," shares Mick, who also owns a renewable energy business that focuses on wind energy system design and education. "The fair has always been a collaboration among business and the renewable energy industry. It's about education, not sales pitches. Even the largest of the manufacturers realize the fair is where it's happening and we're doing what they know needs to be done but don't have the capacity to do."

Adding to the festive atmosphere of the fair, musical entertainers croon on one stage while children create an eco-village out of Legos or make handmade cards out of recycled seed catalogs under another big-top tent. Food vendors feature healthy and delicious meal options while adhering to a strict minimal waste policy that does not allow the use of any disposable packaging. Local farmers sell at a farmers' market, sharing their freshly harvested fruits and vegetables to fair goers to snack on. To accommodate the growing numbers of fair goers on the 20-acre property, the MREA acquired a stand of forest nearby to create the "Back Forty" 250-site campground where, consistent with the rest of the operations, a sustainable forestry plan is in the works.

The fair continues to be the most visible contribution to the growth of the organization and the renewable energy industry. "By virtue of our existence, we have influenced statewide policies and programs," says Katy Matthai, associate director of the MREA. While no accurate measure of renewable energy systems exists on a state or regional basis, sales of systems for business and residential use have mushroomed, with demand outstripping supply. Renewable energy friendly state laws and ample statewide renewable energy and energy conservation incentives encourage the continued growth in systems. And the MREA is right there with the educational resources to back it up.

"There's nothing more empowering than taking your own energy needs into your own hands," concludes Katy. In reality, the MREA has also helped create and support a whole new economic engine in rural areas that restores the land, builds greater local self-reliance for energy and food and nurtures the renewable energy sector that indeed thrives in a life-sustaining economy. "We're all out there trying to save the world and help each other," adds Mick. No fossil fuel needed.

REAP-ING THE BENEFITS OF SUSTAINABILITY
Research, Education, Action, and Policy on Food Group, Madison

For REAP Food Group member Erika Janik, grocery shopping is a revolutionary act. Erika joined the Madison-based group, which stands for Research, Education, Action, and Policy on Food Group, three years ago at the urging of a friend. REAP's express mission is to "build a regional food system that is healthful, just, and both environmentally and economically sustainable."

According to Sustainable Table (www.sustainabletable.org), sustainable agriculture means growing and raising food that is healthy and humane for consumers, animals and workers; does not harm the environment; provides a living wage for farmers; and supports rural communities. This stands in stark contrast to the food lining the shelves of most mainstream grocery stores.

engineering, health, slaughterhouses and processing and others. Buying food with these issues in mind is where the revolutionary part comes in.

Created in 1998 by a small group of citizens interested in how food reaches our tables, REAP initially hosted discussion groups and gave presentations for the public. At that time, several University of Wisconsin faculty members headed REAP. In 1999, the organization branched out to hold the first Food for Thought Festival in Madison. Held each September on Martin Luther King, Jr. Boulevard, the festival boasts speakers, cooking demonstrations, exhibits, live music, children's activities and, of course, food. The annual festival now draws more than 5,000 attendees and more than 50 regional organizations that seek to promote sustainable and local foods.

Conventional wisdom often poses grocery shopping as an exercise in frugality. The idea is to find the lowest prices. However, the prices listed often don't take into account factors such as animal welfare, antibiotics, biodiversity, buying locally, communities and workers, economics, environment, factory farming and the loss of family farms, food irradiation, fossil fuel and energy use, genetic

The recipe contest held as part of the festival receives entries from all over the nation for categories such as Ethnic Heritage, Health and Nutrition, Buying Local, Gardening and Wild-Crafting, Food and Meaning and Kids' Category. Deanna Schneider was the Grand Prize Winner of 2005's recipe contest. Here's how the winning recipe for

Summer Pea Soup emerged in Deanna's own words: "A friend and I do weekly meal swaps with each other and we're constantly challenging each other to do new things with seasonal ingredients. One Saturday we biked up to the farmers' market together and decided that we'd each buy the same ingredients and then go home and prepare something from them. We bought shelled peas, basil, and Capri Farm's goat's milk feta…. It's a very simple soup, best served lukewarm. It tastes like summer in a bowl."

The festival was just the beginning. In 2002, REAP published the Farm Fresh Atlas, a free guide to farms and food-related businesses that sell their goods directly to consumers in southern Wisconsin. With a current distribution of 40,000 copies, the atlas features farms and food businesses that are:

· family or cooperatively owned
· committed to reducing the use of synthetic pesticides and fertilizers
· protecting the region's land and water
· treating their animals with care and respect
· providing safe conditions for their employees
· selling products grown on the farm or produced by the business

Later that year, REAP launched its farm-to-school initiative, Wisconsin Homegrown Lunch. A joint project between REAP and UW-Madison's Center for Integrated Agricultural Systems (CIAS), the program seeks to introduce fresh, nutritious, local and sustainably grown food to the students in Wisconsin's public schools, beginning with elementary school children. In introducing these foods, the program strives to reinvigorate students' connections to their environment, strengthen the relationship between the community and the educational setting, and provide a stable market for local food producers. Moreover, the program obliquely addresses our nation's health crisis. According to the Centers for Disease Control, over the past 20 years, obesity among children has increased by more than

Summer Pea Soup

1 tablespoon olive oil
2 cloves garlic, minced
1 pound (about 3 cups) fresh, shelled green peas
2-3 cups chicken broth or water
3-5 tablespoons heavy cream or half-and-half
1 tablespoon chopped fresh basil
salt and black pepper to taste
goat's milk feta cheese (for garnish)

Heat oil in a sauce pan over medium-low flame, add garlic and briefly sauté it. Add the broth, raise heat and bring to a boil. Reduce heat to medium, add the peas, cover and cook until peas are tender. Check them often and as soon as they're tender, remove pan from the heat. Very fresh peas will need only a few minutes.

Pour peas and broth into a blender. Puree on high until very smooth. You may need to add some extra water at this stage if your peas were not juicy-fresh. Force mixture through a fine sieve. Add chopped basil and cream or half-and-half (if desired). Add salt and pepper to taste. Top each serving with crumbled feta. Makes two large or four small servings.

50 percent, putting these kids at risk for cardiovascular diseases, diabetes and other health problems.

Since its inception, the program has worked with a variety of partners to offer a range of food education lessons through classroom visits by farmers, classroom food "tastings," chef-led cooking lessons and field trips to farms. Since effective food and nutrition education requires making fresh, nutritious food available to children to eat, Wisconsin Homegrown Lunch is providing a fresh, local fruit or vegetable snack to 1,700 students in classrooms at four Madison schools each week. The program also works with numerous school districts that are interested in starting farm-to-school initiatives through their meal programs.

On the Wednesday before the Food for Thought Festival, REAP sponsors the "Local Night Out." On that night, participating restaurants use all local ingredients in at least one dish on their menu. Restaurants from a variety of price ranges participate, so people from all socioeconomic backgrounds can partake of local fare. This speaks to a criticism often leveled at sustainable cuisine: that it is reserved for an elite sector of society. It also challenges restaurants to incorporate sustainably produced ingredients into their menus.

The increasing popularity of all of these programs highlights REAP's greatest achievement in the mind of Executive Director

Miriam Grunes: "Our greatest accomplishment has been to raise the awareness within our community about the importance of creating a strong regional food system."

Even with the heightened awareness, challenges remain. According to Miriam, the industrialized food system still exerts a powerful influence on the way we eat. Despite the presence of many local farmers' markets, community supported agriculture (CSAs) and grocery cooperatives, institutional buyers (like schools and hospitals) find it difficult to purchase directly from farmers. Their budgets are tight, and they've become increasingly reliant on buying "ready-to-serve" foods from a few vendors who can provide all products. REAP hopes to help area farmers meet the needs of these buyers and help institutional buyers purchase locally and sustainably produced food and train employees to prepare whole foods. This will entail expanding regional processing, warehousing and distribution capabilities.

While at first it may seem presumptuous to call grocery shopping "revolutionary," in a way, Erika was right. The choices that we make at our local market link us by invisible threads to countless other people and their livelihoods. It is a subtle and complex revolution. But in subtlety and complexity lie great strength, and REAP Food Group draws on that strength to create a healthy, fair and just food system.

NURTURING LAND, BODIES AND SOULS
Michael Fields Agricultural Institute, East Troy

For over two decades, the innovative Michael Fields Agricultural Institute (MFAI), based in East Troy, has sought out ways to nourish family farms that practice land stewardship, foster a more sustainable food system and bridge the gap between food and farming systems. A primary goal is to bring farmers closer to the people who enjoy the foods they grow. Founded in 1984, the nonprofit organization has spearheaded training programs in organic, sustainable and biodynamic farming, cultivated direct farmer-to-customer sales connections and conducted cutting-edge agricultural research and public policy development.

Within this broad set of goals, MFAI has nurtured numerous projects. Two for-profit businesses now thrive within the arms of the Institute: Fields Best Stores, featuring local and organic produce at both the Milwaukee Public Market and in East Troy, as well as Nokomis Organic Bakery, a natural foods store specializing in artisan breads baked with stone-ground wheat from crops grown at the Institute. The Institute has helped secure year-round vendors for the $12 million Milwaukee Public Market in the city's Historic Third Ward and is launching an ambitious new program designed to turn empty city lots into community gardens of abundance.

"We have always strived to provide solutions to U.S. agricultural problems," explains Ronald Doetch, executive director of MFAI. "When founders Christopher and Martina Mann started the Institute, they wanted to share ways to avoid the plight of agriculture they witnessed in Europe, where not enough food could be grown to support many of the country's own citizens. They envisioned food and farming systems that could be sustainable into perpetuity, and that's what their nonprofit organization set out to accomplish."

The Manns, in partnership with East Troy biodynamic farmer Ruth Zinniker of the Zinniker Dairy Farm—the nation's oldest biodynamic farm—chose to name the Institute after Christopher's affinity for Michael Hall, where he taught for numerous years in his native homeland of Sussex, England. Biodynamic farming practices consider the entire farm as a living organism and recognize the importance of soil, animals, crops and the farm in a balanced and interconnected ecosystem.

"Instead of an indoor classroom, however, Christopher envisioned a place where the future of farming could be taught in a hands-on way in an outdoor classroom," continues Ron. This philosophy, combined with an appreciation for the importance of sustainable food production and biodynamic farming practices, led the Manns to dedicate the five-acre site to serve as training and research grounds. MFAI rents an additional thousand acres from adjacent farmers to conduct research and demonstrate various cropping systems.

Besides the Institute's 8,000-square-foot main building—a Wisconsin barn design with a European flair that houses offices, conference space and a commercial kitchen—the grounds include an 800-square-foot straw bale greenhouse, a 10,000-square-foot conference center facility with housing for students, and a 6.5 kilowatt photovoltaic system with modules on trackers that follow the sun just like the Institute's sunflowers do. Additionally, a 4 kilowatt experimental aerturbines wind system is connected to the roof of the Institute's packing and refrigeration shed. Regular workshops, several intensive seminar series, various farmer training programs and an educational cooking program, "Fields Best Kitchen," featuring a demonstration of local and seasonal ingredients, reach across audiences and build on the common food-agriculture message: we are what we eat.

Much of the first two decades of MFAI's history has focused on producing crop after crop of seasoned new farmers with the honed skills necessary to thrive in the rapidly growing organic and sustainable food sector, conducting research and influencing public policy to support such changes. The Institute is increasingly taking the message and solutions to where the greatest density of people reside—the big cities—while connecting farmers to more profitable market opportunities for their sustainably grown products. "With the expansive growth and interest in organic and sustainably grown foods and fibers, there's a great need in connecting the growers with their customers living in the cities," affirms Ron.

In the Bronzeville neighborhood along the North Avenue of Milwaukee, with many of its residents experiencing some of the most severe unemployment and poverty in the city, MFAI is collaborating with various municipalities, nonprofit organizations, private companies and universities to foster the creation of an energy efficient and "green" retail space. The coalition is also working to transform vacant lots into abundant gardens, encourage localized entrepreneurship and establish safe, healthy common spaces for community members to gather. "All these different departments and agencies were just missing the agricultural puzzle piece, connecting the food problems with economic issues, storm water runoff and sewage spills," Ron admits. "Now the soil is used to raise food for neighborhood residents, to capture storm water that can then be used to irrigate the gardens and to grow veggies that residents can sell to others in the city."

The Institute is jumpstarting an urban agricultural movement that pays local dividends, as Ron explains it, "in the form of local, fresh food, healthier bodies and social and economic development opportunities. We have a systematic problem in inner cities with urban dwellers having little understanding of agriculture and healthy food choices." Having just completed a series of meetings in both Milwaukee and Chicago about transforming city lots into green spots filled with fruits and vegetables, MFAI is becoming a catalyst for urban renewal through food and farmer connections.

"For years, we've held an annual Urban-Rural Food Systems Conference in East Troy. Now were taking it to the city in the form of the Brady Street Artisan Food Festival and we'll expand outreach from a couple hundred attendees to thousands of participants," beams Ron. "We're trying to bring a sustainable food culture to

Milwaukee." The Urban-Rural Food System Conference provides a forum for farmers, individuals, educators, chefs, entrepreneurs and other sustainable agriculture activists to share ideas on how to build a more sustainable, regional food system. Plans are already in the works to continue this expansive outreach effort to create Organic Expos in urban areas throughout the state in the coming years.

Listening to the people who want fresh, seasonal, local and organic food has become the new marketing mantra advocated by MFAI. "The nonprofit world has increasingly become market driven," Ron notes. "Therefore, we're driving the program from a marketing perspective as opposed to a production focus where farmers ended up growing what they wanted to grow. We need our farmers to produce what the customers want to buy. Our role is to help connect farmers to their customers." The two Fields Best stores that feature seasonal, local and sustainable fruits, vegetables and herbs are the flowering new centerpieces for MFAI. The more their farmers and their Fields Best stores prosper, the greater the future funding for further expansion of the programs.

Years of involvement on both state and federal levels have also paid off for the Institute, resulting in a major victory for family farms. Partnering with the USDA's Natural Resource Conservation Service and Farm Service Agency, MFAI joined forces with other organizations to help craft the Conservation Security Program, or CSP, where the government is willing to pay for good stewardship practices regardless of size of farm or type of crop raised. "The new CSP allows farmers to supply real food now because that's what the farmer is getting paid for," Ron explains.

Some of Michael Fields' other activities are also finding footing. "Years of research under the direction of Dr. Walter Goldstein have begun to reveal opportunities for sustainable growers. Soon to be banned for certified organic farms, a synthetic Methionine, which is needed by chickens, can also be naturally found in certain cultivars of corn, according to Walter's findings," shares Ron, offering it as an organic alternative to poultry rations with synthetic inputs. "And Michael Fields' outreach to conventional farmers has continued as well, since we're not going to change the way chemical-based farming is practiced if we're not talking with them."

As a catalyst for bringing forth conversations around food, Michael Fields Agricultural Institute is springing forward with an abundance of programs fostering the very connections required for individuals and whole cities to rediscover the culture of agriculture and its importance to nurturing the land, our bodies, our souls and our common future.

AFTERWORD

Renewing the Countryside—Wisconsin has been several years in the making. The story behind the book is reflective of the stories featured within it—filled with vision, creativity and pursuit of a better world.

The first book entitled *Renewing the Countryside* was produced in the Netherlands by that country's Ministry of Agriculture. It was an atlas of sustainable initiatives throughout the Dutch countryside and inspired the creation of similar publications and a nonprofit of the same name here in the U.S. *Renewing the Countryside* books have been produced in Minnesota, Iowa, North Dakota, Washington and the Four Corners region of the Southwest.

The seed for the Wisconsin book did not take root in a single spot, but rather in the fertile minds of several people. Each of these people—individually—contacted Renewing the Countryside to determine how to make this project happen in Wisconsin. After several phone calls and meetings, these partners joined forces to undertake the fundraising, research, management and implementation of the project. They have all contributed creative energy, knowledge and many hours of time.

One of these people, Mary Rehwald, a sustainability advocate and Ashland City Council member, saw the Minnesota *Renewing the Countryside* book and immediately set off to make a comparable project happen in Wisconsin. At the time, she oversaw summer programs at Northland College and was able to develop a summer course in which students, under the instruction of professional writers and photographers, went out and captured the stories and photos of local businesses and farms that were leaders in living and working sustainably. A number of those stories are included in this book, and all of them made their way into a booklet published by the class.

At about the same time, Faye Jones, executive director at the Midwest Organic and Sustainable Education Service (MOSES), was exploring this idea too—having talked with one of the organizers in Minnesota. The staff at MOSES not only knew most of the innovative farmers in the state, they also had their annual Upper Midwest Organic Farming Conference, which has served as a venue for gathering input for the book. One of MOSES' invaluable contributions to this project has been the participation of Jody Padgham, their education director, who has served as editor, writer and an endless source of information.

Finally, Jerry Hembd, director of the Northern Center for Community and Economic Development at the University of Wisconsin-Superior, bid on and won a copy of one of the *Renewing the Countryside* books at a silent auction. He too saw the value of doing a similar project in Wisconsin and how it would fit naturally with the work of his center. Jerry has served as an editor for this project, wrote one of the stories and called on his colleagues at the University of Wisconsin-Extension to gather story ideas and to produce some of the pieces in this book.

The soul of this book comes from the stories of the amazing people who are showcased here. We were able to capture that soul through the extraordinary talent of a team of artists and writers. The art direction, design and production of this book came from the gifted hand of Brett Olson, creative director at Renewing the Countryside.

John Ivanko and Lisa Kivirist wrote over a third of the stories, and John brought those stories further to life with his award-wining photography. John and Lisa found and contacted Renewing the Countryside several years ago and a lovely friendship and partnership has ensued. They were early advocates for a *Renewing the Countryside—Wisconsin* book to showcase the amazing array of activities happening in the state.

A number of other talented writers contributed to this book. They include: Lorene Anderson, Mark Fondriest, Jo Futrell, Meg Gores, Ann Hanson, Erika Linn Janik, Mary Rehwald, Michelle Shaw and Bill Wright. One of the writers, Ann Hanson, introduced us to her nephew, Tom Baker, newly graduated from the University of Montana School of Journalism. Tom not only captured amazing photographs for the stories he was assigned, he also turned these photo shoots around in record time. A number of other photographers shared their talents, and they are acknowledged in the photo credits.

At the Renewing the Countryside headquarters, Lindsay Rehban, Margaret Schnieders and Monica Siems provided invaluable assistance. We owe a special thanks to the crew at University of Wisconsin Press who are as excited about this book as we are and helping us to get it into the hands of as many people as possible.

In an ideal world, a book like this would be wildly profitable (or at least cover its costs)! The truth is that regional, photo-filled books are very expensive to produce and in order to make this book affordable and get it into the hands of educators and other key people, we needed to rely on the generosity of supporters. Renewing the Countryside received funding from the W.K. Kellogg Foundation to collect a number of the stories featured in this book. The Kellogg Foundation's commitment to rural America is extraordinary and we thank them for their support. The Brico Fund, a farsighted Wisconsin Foundation with a commitment to systems change, provided core funding that put this project into high gear.

Finally, we want to thank the individuals featured in the stories. Not only for what they do, but also for working with the writers, photographers and editors to make this publication possible. We also want to thank all the other individuals, families and businesses working to renew Wisconsin's countryside that we were unable to include in this volume. We could only showcase a fraction of the great examples of rural renewal and whittling the list down to a couple dozen examples was painful. In the end, we aimed for a broad and diverse representation.

We hope you will take the time to search out the sustainable gems in your area. All of the organizations involved in this project can help you find them, as well as information and resources for pursuing your own enterprise or initiative. Our goal is to support innovative, sustainable development in rural communities in every way possible.

Sincerely,

Jan Joannides, Series Editor

PUBLISHING PARTNERS

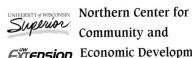 **Midwest Organic and Sustainable Education Service**

The Midwest Organic and Sustainable Education Service (MOSES) is dedicated to helping farmers and others understand and support sustainable and organic agriculture. A nonprofit 501(c)3 institution, MOSES operates in a seven-state region from a headquarters in rural Spring Valley, WI. The organization does outreach and education through ongoing projects, activities and collaborations with partners throughout the region.

Primary projects include an annual Upper Midwest Organic Farming Conference, attended by 2,300 in 2007, and a comprehensive website offering a current calendar of events, online service directory, numerous informative fact sheets about organic production and certification and more. MOSES also publishes the Organic Broadcaster Newspaper six times per year and undertakes a diversity of special trainings on organic certification and production directed at farmers and educators.

For more information, visit the MOSES website at www.mosesorganic.org.

 Northern Center for Community and Economic Development

The Northern Center for Community and Economic Development (NCCED) supports community and economic development in northern Wisconsin through applied research, education and outreach. It is a joint effort between the University of Wisconsin-Superior and the University of Wisconsin-Extension. The Center is housed on the UW-Superior campus in the Department of Business and Economics. The Center's staff is part of the statewide Community, Natural Resource and Economic Development (CNRED) program area of UW-Extension.

Over the past few years, efforts at the Center have been focused on the areas of sustainability, rural and community development, the creative economy, and regional economic analysis. The Center also works in support of statewide educational emphases in four broad areas: economic development, natural resources, leadership and organizational development, and local government. As a regional center, it works directly with multicounty and statewide organizations and agencies on issues of specific importance to northern Wisconsin.

For more information about the Center and its activities and for links to the resources of the University of Wisconsin-Superior and the University of Wisconsin-Extension, go to the NCCED website at www.uwsuper.edu/ncced.

Renewing the Countryside

Renewing the Countryside (RTC) is a Minnesota-based nonprofit organization that works with partners from across the country to collectively share stories of people who are redefining what it means to live, work and learn in rural America. These stories provide hope, inspiration, and ideas for building strong, sustainable rural communities.

Through the generous support of individuals and foundations, Renewing the Countryside is dedicated to sharing the strength of America's rural landscape: the people enhancing their cultural and natural resources while spurring local economic development in their communities.

To read more stories of people revitalizing their rural communities, visit the Renewing the Countryside website at www.renewingthecountryside.org.

STORY MAP

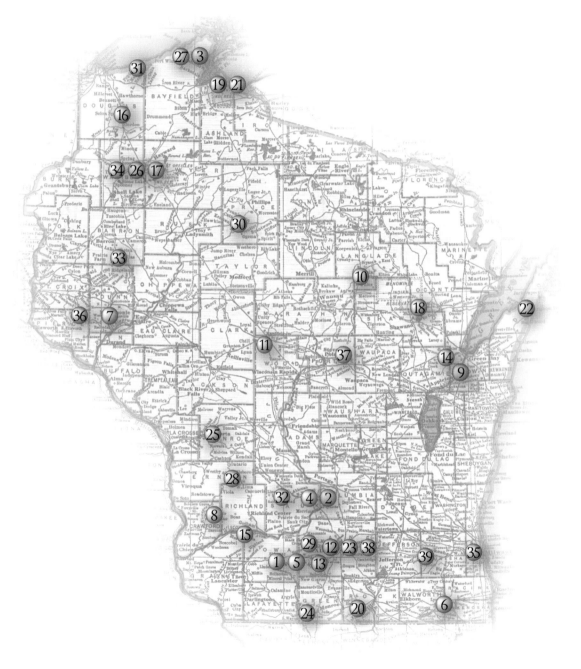

1. Folklore Village, Dodgeville, p. 14-17
   608.924.4000
   www.folklorevillage.org

2. Baraboo Valley Windsor Chairs, Rock Springs,
   p. 18-21
   608.393.3347
   www.baraboovalleywindsors.com

3. Lake Superior Big Top Chautauqua, Bayfield,
   p. 22-24
   888.244.8368
   www.bigtop.org

4. The Wormfarm Institute, Reedsburg, p. 25-28
   608-524-8672
   www.wormfarminstitute.org

5. Fall Art Tour, Mineral Point, Spring Green,
   Dodgeville and Baraboo, p. 29-31
   608.588.7906
   www.fallarttour.com

6. Krusen Grass Farm, Elkhorn, p. 34-36
   262.642.7312
   www.krusengrassfarms.com

7. Bullfrog Fish Farm, Menomonie, p. 37-39
   715.664.8775
   www.eatmyfish.com

8. Turkey Ridge Organic Apple Orchard, Gays Mills,
   p. 40-42
   608.735.4661
   www.turkeyridgeorganic.com

9. The Strenn Farm, Greenleaf, p. 43-45

10. Igl Farms, Antigo. p. 46-49

11. Good Earth Farms, Marshfield, p. 51-53
    888.941.4343
    www.goodearthfarms.com

12. Dane County Farmers' Market, Madison, p. 56-59
    www.dcfm.org

13. Vermont Valley Community Farm, Blue Mounds
    p. 60-63
    608.767.3860,
    www.vermontvalley.com

14. Tsyunhehkwa Center, Oneida, p. 64-66

15. Ho-Chunk Nation, Muscoda, p. 67-69
    608.739.3360
    www.muscodabison.com

16. Lucius Woods Performing Arts Center, Solon Springs,
    p. 70-73
    715.378.4272
    www.lwmusic.org

17. WOJB, Lac Courte Oreilles Band of the
    Lake Superior Ojibwe, Hayward, p. 74-77
    715.634.2100
    www.wojb.org

18. Menominee Tribal Enterprises, Keshena, p. 80-82
    715.756.2311
    www.mtewood.com

19. Northland College, Ashland, p. 83-85
    715.682.1699
    www.northland.edu

20. Applied Ecological Services, Brodhead, p. 86-89
    608.897.3641
    www.appliedeco.com

21. Eco-Municipalities on Chequamegon Bay,
    Ashland, Bayfield and bay area, p. 90-92

22. Lake Michigan Wind and Sun, Sturgeon Bay,
    p. 93-95
    920.743.0456
    www.windandsun.com

23. The Ice Age Trail, crossing Wisconsin, p. 98-101
    800.227.0046
    www.iceagetrail.org

24. Inn Serendipity Bed & Breakfast, Browntown,
    p. 102-105
    608.329.7056
    www.innserendipity.com

25. Justin Trails Resort, Sparta, p. 106-108
    608.269.4522
    www.justintrails.com

26. Wisconsin's Northwest Heritage Passage,
    p. 109-111
    715.635.6811
    www.heritagepassage.com

27. Pinehurst Inn at Pikes Creek Bed & Breakfast,
    Bayfield, p. 112-115
    877.499.7651
    www.pinehurstinn.com

28. Organic Valley Family of Farms, La Farge,
    p. 118-121
    608.625.2602
    www.organicvalley.coop

29. Cedar Grove Cheese, Plain, p. 122-124
    800.200.6020
    www.cedargrovecheese.com

30. Wisconsin Sheep Dairy Co-op, Catawba and
    beyond, p. 125-127
    www.sheepmilk.biz

31. White Winter Winery, Iron River, p. 129-131
    800.697.2006
    www.whitewinter.com

32. Willow Creek Farm, Loganville, p. 132-134
    608.727.2224
    www.willowcreekpork.com

33. Viking Brewery, Dallas, p. 135-137
    715.837.1824
    www.vikingbrewing.com

34. Crystal Creek, Trego, p. 138-140
    888.376.6777
    www.crystalcreeknatural.com

35. Growing Power, Milwaukee. p. 144-148
    414.527.1546
    www.growingpower.org

36. Midwest Organic and Sustainable Education
    Service, Spring Valley, p. 148-150
    715.772.3153
    www.mosesorganic.org

37. Midwest Renewable Energy Association, Custer,
    p. 151-153
    715.592.6595
    www.the-mrea.org

38. Research, Education, Action, and
    Policy on Food Group, Madison, p. 154-156
    www.reapfoodgroup.org

39. Michael Fields Agricultural Institute, East Troy,
    p. 157-159
    262.642.3303
    www.michaelfieldsaginst.org

STORY CREDITS
WRITERS & PHOTOGRAPHERS

COVER

Photography: *Wisconsin Sunset*, Tom Baker; *Herby Radman, Eat My Fish Platter*, Tom Baker; *Boy in Field*, © Carrie Branovan for Organic Valley; *Boy with Calf*, © Carrie Branovan for Organic Valley; *Home Grown Culture Pea Pod*, Sandy Weisz; *Lori Taguma, general manager of WOJB*, Tom Baker; Inside front flap: *Vermont Valley Rough Housing*, Will Ringland; Spine: *Happy Piggy*, Tom Baker; Back Cover: *Olivia and the Hen*, Brett Olson.

TITLE

Photography: p.2 - *Three bales*, Brett Olson.

COPYRIGHT

Photography: p.5 - *Wood Lake*, Eric Sherman.

FOREWORD

Writer: Governor Jim Doyle
Photography: p.8 - *Country girl*, Sandy Weisz; p.9 - *Governor Jim Doyle*.

INTRODUCTION

Writers: Jerry Hembd, Jan Joannides, Faye Jones, Jody Padgham and Mary Rehwald.
Photography: p.11 - *Sunset over lake*, Brett Olson.

ARTS & CULTURE

Introduction: Jody Padgham
Photography: p.12 - *Ramon Lopez Anders painting hay bales*, Donna Neuwirth; p.13 - *Band under the tent*, Dave Obey; p.13 - *Steven Spiro console table*, Courtesy Steven Spiro.

WEAVING A CULTURAL TAPESTRY

FOLKLORE VILLAGE, DODGEVILLE

Writer: Meg Gores
Photography: p.15 - *Woman and child weaving*, Dick Aimsworth; p.16 - *Wagon ride through prairie*, Melissa Leef; p.17 - *Maypole Dance*, Doug Miller.

TIMELESS FURNITURE

BARABOO VALLEY WINDSOR CHAIRS, ROCK SPRINGS

Writers: Lisa Kivirist & John Ivanko
Photography: p.18 - *David Ogren with spindle*, John Ivanko; p.19 - *Windsor chair parts*, Courtesy of Dave Ogren; p.21 - *Baraboo Valley Windsor chair*, John Ivanko.

UNDER THE BIG TENT

LAKE SUPERIOR BIG TOP CHAUTAUQUA, BAYFIELD

Writer: Lorene Anderson
Photography: p.23 - *Big Top Chatauqua tent*, Courtesy of Lake Superior Big Top Chatauqua; p.24 - *Blue Canvas Orchestra and Singers*, Courtesy of Lake Superior Big Top Chatauqua.

PUTTING CULTURE BACK IN AGRICULTURE

THE WORMFARM INSTITUTE, REEDSBURG

Writer: Lisa Kivirist & John Ivanko
Photography: p.25 - *Regin drawing*, Donna Neuwirth; p.26 - *Tim Stankovitz at the Wormcastings Foundry*, Donna Neuwirth; p.27 - *Beth in the garden*, Donna Neuwirth; p.28 - *Home Grown Culture Band*, Sandy Weisz.

THE FALL ART TOUR

MINERAL POINT, SPRING GREEN, DODGEVILLE AND BARABOO

Writers: Lisa Kivirist & John Ivanko
Photography: p.29 - *Fall Road*, Courtesy of The Fall Art Tour; p.30 - *JorJan Borlin working on a bead loom with Coa Coa*, Peter Schwei; p.31- left to right, *The Standout by Diana Johnston*, Doug Miller; *Garnet ring with gold and silver by Wayne Farra*, Larry Sanders; *Console table by Steven Spiro*, Steven Spiro; *"Opening" in porcelain by Sandra Byers*, Sandra Byers.

INNOVATIVE FARMING

Introduction: Jody Padgham
Photography: p.32 - *Misty spring morning*, Brett Olson; p.33 - *Happy CSA member*, Will Ringland; *Bullfrog fish pond*, Tom Baker.

SWEET ORGANIC PASTURED PROFITS

KRUSEN GRASS FARM, ELKHORN

Writers: Lisa Kivirist & John Ivanko
Photography: p.34 - *Cows with double rainbow*, Altfrid Krusenbaum; p.35 - *Krusenbaum family*, John Ivanko.

EAT MY FISH

BULLFROG FISH FARM, MENOMONIE

Writer: Ann Hanson
Photography: p.37 - *Herby Radmann with fish*, Tom Baker; p.38 - *Families fishing*, Tom Baker.

ACRES OF APPLES AND MORE

TURKEY RIDGE ORGANIC APPLE ORCHARD, GAYS MILLS

Writers: Lisa Kivirist & John Ivanko
Photography: p.41 - *Alex Person, Faye Rogers and Jahmuna*, John Ivanko; p.42 - *Orchard and blue bird box*, John Ivanko.

INDEX

Bold text indicates photographs